I

1 Spencer Street Railway Station
2 Head Offices, Railway Depart-
  ment
3 Customs House
4 Central Railway Station
5 Princes Bridge Railway Station
6 Anglican Cathedral
7 State Public Offices
8 Masonic Hall
9 Government Tourist Bureau
10 Athenæum Hall
11 Town Hall
12 Federal Parliament House
13 Princess Theatre

22 Law Courts
23 Titles and Registrar-General's
   Office
24 Public Library, Museum and Art
   Gallery
25 Royal Mint

Tramways shown thus ═══

BY THE SAME AUTHOR

TID *(a case history)*

CHINESE DRAMA IN THE GOLDFIELDS *(a treatise)*

THE BLUE LAMINGTON *(a novel)*

BIZARRE *(a compilation)*

THE WONDERFUL WORLD OF
BARRY MCKENZIE *(a comic strip)*

BARRY HUMPHRIES' BOOK OF
INNOCENT AUSTRAL VERSE *(an anthology)*

DAME EDNA'S COFFEE TABLE BOOK *(a compendium)*

A TREASURY OF AUSTRALIAN KITSCH *(an excavation)*

LES PATTERSON'S AUSTRALIA *(a panegyric)*

A NICE NIGHT'S ENTERTAINMENT *(a retrospective)*

THE DAME EDNA BEDSIDE COMPANION *(a soporific)*

THE TRAVELLER'S TOOL *(a manual)*

MY GORGEOUS LIFE *(an adventure)*

THE LIFE AND DEATH OF SANDY STONE *(an obituary)*

NEGLECTED POEMS
BARRY HUMPHRIES
AND OTHER CREATURES

Angus&Robertson
An imprint of HarperCollins*Publishers*

AN ANGUS & ROBERTSON BOOK
An imprint of HarperCollinsPublishers

First published in Australia in 1991 by
CollinsAngus&Robertson Publishers Pty Limited (ACN 009 913 517)
A division of HarperCollinsPublishers (Australia) Pty Limited
25-31 Ryde Road, Pymble NSW 2073 Australia

HarperCollins Publishers (New Zealand) Limited
31 View Road, Glenfield, Auckland 10, New Zealand

HarperCollins Publishers Limited
77-85 Fulham Palace Road, London W6 8JB, United Kingdom

Copyright © International Services Ltd 1991

This book is copyright.
Apart from any fair dealing for the purposes of private study,
research, criticism or review, as permitted under the Copyright
Act, no part may be reproduced by any process without written
permission. Inquiries should be addressed to the publishers.

National Library of Australia
Cataloguing-in-Publication data:

Humphries, Barry, 1934–
   Neglected Poems.

    ISBN 0 207 17212 9

    I. Title

A821.3

Cover photograph courtesy of the Melbourne Herald
Printed in Australia by Griffin Press

5   4   3   2   1
95 94 93 92 91

With love to
SMALLCAPS STEPHEN SPENDER

A sprig of gum leaves
In homage
To your bays.

ACKNOWLEDGEMENTS

The authors all wish to thank the following:

Stanley Brown, for early encouragement; Peter Coleman, friend and memorialist; Keith Dunstan, for so generously publishing so much of these occasional verses in his newspaper column over many years; Katherine Brisbane and John Allen, for reprinting some of these stanzas in *The Humour of Barry Humphries* and *A Nice Night's Entertainment* (Currency Press); and *Private Eye* and *Quadrant* for permission to reproduce verse which originally appeared under their imprints.

We would especially like to thank our present editor Louise Thurtell, publisher Tom Thompson and designer Alison Windmill at Collins/Angus&Robertson.

CONTENTS

Sir Les Patterson

PROLEGOMENON

While yet a schoolboy I discovered how magically even the crudest rhyme and metre could transform ideas of the utmost bathos. The most banal perceptions, which, if couched in prose would bring ridicule upon their author, assume an aura of bogus subtlety, sapience and even wit when tricked up as 'poems'.

I began writing verses early in life; won poetry prizes at a school where there was very little competition in artistic fields, and even had a few stanzas, heavily bowdlerised, published in the school magazine. Re-reading these with a shudder today, I see the ill-digested influences of my early poetic idols: Francis Thompson, Siegfried Sassoon and the Sitwells. Earnest, soul-searching juvenilia they are. The themes of pacifism, theological doubt and clammy pubescent yearning jostle each other in verses with titles like 'Futility', 'Lament from the Tomb' and 'Failure'.

At the same time, however, under the spell of Edith Sitwell's *Façade* and some of Osbert's verse satires, I was developing a more flippant tone. A Sitwellian pastiche from 1950 survives.

> *In Portobello hear Othello bellow*
> *Blacker than a telephone*
> *For the Moor has espied his tobacco-coloured bride*
> *Being taken for a ride upon a billow*
> *While firm in the ermine embrace of a merman*
> *His wife is determined to stay*
> *Like a nymph in a Rape she tries not to escape*
> *As they romp in the crêpe de Chine bay*
> *Then black as a telephone bellows Othello*
> *O'er the willow-blue water of Portobello*

While his chocolate toe, as cute as Canute's
Tempts the iced-cider tide to flow over his boots
Then Othello awoke with a yell as the yoke
Of the sun fell and broke in the ocean
As mellow as Milton the moon's yellow Stilton
Arose like a soul to salvation
So farewell Othello old fellow
We never shall see thee again
May you dance all your rhumbas at the Cafe Columbus
For ever and ever Amen!

This early 'rap' and similar ditties were delivered as late night party turns to the accompaniment of loud Latin American music on the gramophone. Dame Edith was never aware of her antipodean rival.

The pacifist theme occurred in another verse of this period called *The Four Horsemen of the Apocalypse*. These are the only lines I can remember since two of the horses appear to have bolted:

Mounted on cloven castanets
With epileptic epaulettes
The genial General devises
International surprises

Meanwhile the man who makes the guns
And profits on conscripted sons
Laments the public are such gluttons
For commemorative buttons.

Anti-jingoistic jingles such as this read rather like minor contributions to *Oxford Poetry 1924*, and could be atavistic parodies of the early Harold Acton.

At Melbourne University my poetic output slowed down. This was my Dadaist period and the clever assonances and alliterations of the Sitwell/Sassoon epoch yielded to a more misanthropic voice.

2

One day an old lady sniffed a rose
And a large dark insect entered her nose
No sooner had she recovered from this unprovoked attack
Than she tripped on the drive and broke her back.

Child abuse and parental savagery were also persistent themes in my lyrics of the early 1950s.

My child erred,
I chid it
The doctor said:
Who did it?

Or

I struck my son
The little devil
Now his eyes
Never look level.

These cautionary verses and many others in the same paedophobic vein, were gleefully recorded by members of the Wubbo Movement — or the Melbourne Dadaist Chapter. A gramophone recording was published in a minutely limited edition and is now of the very last rarity, since most of the Wubboists involved now hold High Office and could be embarrassed were their constituents, parishioners, congregations and grandchildren to hear their youthful voices intoning:

My daughter kissed me
With childlike grace
So I bit all the skin
Off the front of her face!

With uncanny prescience these lines anticipate by nearly forty years the central *donnée* of popular entertainments like *The Silence of the Lambs*.

In the mid-1950s I joined a theatrical troupe and

invented the character of Mrs Everage, Moonee Ponds housewife and recent winner of the Lovely Mother Contest. Dressed in a dowdy twin-set, plastic pearls and yellow conical hat and with a voice of fluting gentility, Mrs Everage, in her earliest stage incarnation, was much given to recitation. 'Maroan' (QV) was amongst her earliest theatrical successes, but over the years, as she grew in popularity and in her own estimation, few occasions went by which she did not commemorate in verse. A selection of Dame Edna's tirades and panegyrics are reprinted in this volume with her gracious permission. Many of them refer to events and personages long forgotten and the reader may find the notes at the end of the book useful in illuminating obscure topical references and other recondites.

In the early seventies, before she was invested with a Damehood by the Right Honourable Gough Whitlam, Mrs Everage was still slightly prim and xenophobic, and in her pioneering and proto-Green *Ode to Maid Melbourne* she makes pejorative and discriminatory remarks about the odour of 'New Australians' which she would deplore in 1991. In more recent years she has been called upon to perform such diverse official functions as opening the Harrods annual sale and switching on the Christmas lights in Regent Street, London. On all of these occasions, whether eulogising a radio announcer or anathematising her bridesmaid, Dame Edna has expressed herself poetically, and it is as well, when reading her verses baldly printed on the page, to imagine the Dame herself enunciating these measures in her inimitable style; rolling the words across her palate like forkfuls of pavlova.

The loutish, albeit innocent Barry McKenzie, lantern-jawed progenitor of Crocodile Dundee, was a creature of the sixties when Fosters Lager was an obscure Melbourne beverage only obtainable at one disreputable pub in London. McKenzie's adventures in Earl's Court were chronicled throughout the decade in a comic strip in the fortnightly lampoon, *Private Eye*, and in the early seventies, in two successful motion pictures directed by Bruce Beresford. Barry McKenzie's esoteric taste for Fosters beer and his inability to retain it for any length of time, led to many protests from the embarrassed brewer, but by 1980 Fosters had become almost universally known and distributed, due entirely to Barry's persistent advocacy. Even television advertisements for the frothy cordial began to feature craggy-faced Australians wearing hats, and laconic references to 'cracking tinnies' and 'ice-cold tubes'.

From time to time Barry McKenzie burst into song, and the text of his legendary balnearic *The Old Pacific Sea*, which extols for the first time in the history of the Race the pleasures of 'chundering', is herein reprinted. The lyrics of some of McKenzie's songs also appear on these pages, but divorced from their music, they lack much of their original charm and impact.

Perhaps the most vigorous and authentically Australian voice represented in this anthology belongs to the quondam cultural Attaché to the Court of St. James, Chairman of the Australian Chapter of the International Cheese Board, Patron of the Thursday Island Film Commission and Editor Emeritus of the Oxford Companion to Australian Literature, Doctor Sir Leslie Colin Patterson. A prolific versifier, with that instinctive command of the demotic which is the birthright of all Australians, Dr Patterson is represented by innumerable odes and occasional poems embracing all aspects of antipodean life. Always outspoken, even, at times

Fescennine, his work is firmly in the 'larrikin' tradition of Australian proletarian literature, which stretches back through C. J. Dennis, Henry Lawson and Sir Leslie's poetic namesake 'Banjo' Paterson to the bush balladeers of the nineteenth century. Little wonder that in spite of his occasional lapses into bawdy, the good humour, virility and above all the patriotism of his verse has found a firm place in the hearts of the men, women and children of Oceania.

My own contribution to this book is a comparatively modest one. The Reader is spared my pessimistic *juvenilia* but I have been persuaded by my Editor to publish pasquinades from the sixties and assorted doggerel and facetiae from the seventies and eighties, as well as some occasional verse and nostalgic lucubrations in which the influences of John Betjeman and William Plomer may sometimes obtrude.

At least three-quarters of the verse in this volume was written for public recitation, where inconsistencies in rhyme and metre can be cunningly elided. It was never intended that they should be divorced from the authorial voice or outlive their ephemeral purpose and appear on the printed page. They have been reprieved here in the hope that they will amuse, and cast a fitful light on contemporary prejudices, fashionable jargon, and withal, on the Author's more cherished and persistent bugbears. Again, the Notes may help the Reader identify many references to persons and events lost long ago in the penumbra of time.

BARRY HUMPHRIES
CARLTON HILL STATION
EAST KIMBERLEY
WESTERN AUSTRALIA
JULY 1991

▪ BARRY ▪

HUMPHRIES

THE BALLAD OF
CHARLES BLACKMAN[1]

for Victoria Blackman

The autumn gales blow sharp and shrill
From Ladbroke Grove to Highgate Hill,
From Cricklewood to Pimlico
And down the darksome tubes they blow.
They blow the Kellogg's coloured leaves
About these high pagoda'd eaves[2]
In Chinese market gardens hear
The stealthy breath of Autumn sere.
Rustling the bamboos and the celery
Like chequebooks in Mattiesen's Gallery,
Where the art patrons, wise and rich
Behold Charles Blackman's work and itch
To pay large monies that they might
Own three square yards of masonite,
On which the aforesaid Charles did toil
To decorate with coal and oil.

Time was when riotous jungles stood
From Shepherd's Bush to Highgate Wood,
And this the earth did swallow whole,
Converting trees to oil and coal . . .
Charles, like a miner, only greedier,

9

Raids these deep chasms[3] for his media.
What manner then of man is this,
Whose light winks in the world's abyss?
His physique — I'll describe it easily;
He is the easel's Scobie Breasley.
Like jockeys are, he's short and thinnish,
Each picture is a photo-finish.

Boyd paints brides in their newly-wed clothes
But Blackman takes us under the bed clothes
Where slowly we descry the shapes
Of hands and noses, hats and napes.

Fingers and flowers, hanks of hair,
Caught in a subterranean flare —

Before I bid you praise our host
And charge your glasses for a toast.
One further tribute I would make
Ere we do this libation take;
It is a point sage Bryan[4] has seen,
And yet it bears repeat, I ween:
Charles Blackman's *blacks* deserve our praise,
And to a less extent, his greys.
And so I say with all my heart
Three cheers for Charles
His name is Black
He is the Sweep of Art!

1961

BOYD SONG
AT EVENTIDE[1]

for Yvonne Boyd

TO BE RECITED IN ELDRITCH TONES

Winter has whitened London like a clown
The trees are birds' claws buried upside down
Behind occasional windows dim with steam
Hot casseroles of people dance and scream,
Laundrettes of laughter spin the drip-dry folk,
Inhaling beer and gulping pints of smoke.
Outside the icebergs of disaster cruise
On the lookout for pleasure boats to bruise.
Long whiles agone in one such glassy street,
The cobbles rang with Jack the Ripper's feet,
Behold what this grim artist left behind:
A large nude in vermilion — unsigned.
Few artists, we must own, have done so well
Since that bleak winter's night in Whitechapel
Yet there be one, methinks, will fill the void
I mean God wot, young Arthur Merric Boyd!
For when the Spring breaks winter's icy spell
His art will burst like buds in Whitechapel.
Not since the coming of the dinosaur
Will men have known so lithe and lush a Thaw

11

Europe will hasten to the Aldgate Road
Beholding there a huge and emerald toad
And evolution will change perspective
When Arthur Merric holds his Retrospective.

■   ■   ■

Lofty white windmills like young brides will faint
And fan the bracken with their stricken sails
Gazing in pools where goldfish swim like paint
Through deeps as membranous as bridal veils.
Large luminous dogs will look with mild reproach
As the pavilion'd elders darkly stare;
Susannah wears her nipple like a brooch!
Blossoms will trickle through the blushing air
The hairy hillsides climb towards the snow
A ram comes blundering out with a spiral horn
High in a gnawed white tree, there sits the crow
And in the dark the bridegroom's dream is born.
The beetle ticks upon the murderer's cheek
The lovers drown like swimmers in the grass
They gaze into the earth and what they seek
We pray that the dark earth will bring to pass.

ENVOI

When Spring hits frozen Europe once again
Take the whole family down to Petticoat Lane.
And when the nippers ask *what's on the go?*
Tell them it's Arthur Merric's One Man Show
                                        1962

AN ODE TO THE CITY OF CAMBERWELL[1]

for Barbara Johnson

To hear Thy name, my memory strays
Back to sweet far-off childhood days
When Camberwell was still a town,
And the Old Rivoli burned down.
Survivor of more recent fire
Is old St John's brave red-brick spire.
Oh Camberwell! Your parks, your shops,
War Savings Streets and tramway stops;
Your famous Junction with its web
Of wires above; below the ebb
And flow of busy shopping mothers;
Braithwaite the Chemist, Adair Brothers,
The Six Ways Milk Bar; and of yore,
Smileaway Sweet Shop — now no more!
Woolworths and Coles, Trengroves for shoes,
The 'Broadway' where you bought Screen News,
The Market too, a feast of odours:
Gladdy bulbs and creamy sodas,
Glen Valley Tea and Maxam Cheese,
Fresh schnapper, stocks, phlox and sweet peas.
And Adam's Cake Shop, paradise
Of honey roll, vanilla slice

And rainbow terrace — Gee I'm hungry!
But don't you remember the fishmongery
With water waving down the glass,
And butcher's artificial grass?
Sawdusted floor, upon which you
(While mummy shopped) discreetly drew
Childish designs with Bedgegood shoe.

Riversdale Road will yet abide
As the great route to swing and slide;
And when at last the tramline ended —
There was Wattle Park extended!
Golden trees, grass-tufted shade
Where cabbage moths and children played,
Families with thermoses and prams,
And derelict old cable trams!
I went back there not long ago
And saw how Time had changed it so;
It looked so moth-eaten and bare,
And yet, miraculously, still there!
What tidy lawns, what cream brick slums
Could have replaced those scarred old gums?
But knowing Melbourne, it's not too late —
There'll be a Wattle Park Estate!

But think on things which are no more:
No tradesmen trudge from door to door;
When I was young a Chink with veges
A bicycling Russian trimmed the hedges

And I recall an ice-cream cart well —
And matinees at the Regal Hartwell,
Now a Service Station — Why?
The Regal was too young to die!
Oh Camberwell Town Hall look down
On this your City, once a town,
And then, before that, vacant blocks
Where no-one thought of planning phlox
Or building Ampol petrol bowsers
Or stucco'd Spanish Mission houses.
Yet ever in my mind you'll dwell —
Hideous, heartbreaking Camberwell,
And ere I take Extremest Unction
My Soul will flash back to 'The Junction'.

1968

UNTITLED SONG
FOR THE SIXTIES

When I was just a kiddie filled with thick sweet Saunder's Malt
I used to ask the driver of our Oldsmobile to halt,
And pointing to a terrace house I'd ask my dad and mum:
'Oh please, PLEASE let me go inside, I've never seen a slum!'
'Some of those homes aren't real slums,' my paternal chauffeur cried,
'It just depends how scrupulous the people are inside.
I've seen a few homes worse than that in suburbs just as poor,
But with windows clean and shiny like the brass knob on the door.'

■   ■   ■

Now, thirty years have passed us by, most of the slums are
     wrecked,
And those remaining house photographer and architect.
They're painted black or grey or green, their lacework picked
     out white,
And their parties and their stereos play late into the night.
Their rich young long-haired owners are real patrons of the
     Arts.
You've never heard more Hendrix, never seen such big Pro
     Harts!
A while ago, I went to one, and wondered what a guest meant
When he said to Peter Jason, 'What a beautiful investment!'

I noticed on the wall there was a crucified Koala.
'What's that called Pete?' The host said gravely 'Untitled
   Mandala'.
Another 'good investment' was some three-ply painted blue,
The host said it was called 'Untitled Painting Number Two'.
'Untitled Triptych' covered five square yards of masonite,
Said Peter Jason's guest: 'You've got a gold mine there all
   right.'
Our flattered host then led us to the bedroom of his house,
And we gazed in awe-struck silence at 'Untitled Mickey
   Mouse'.
'It really should light up,' he said, 'except there's one slight
   hitch,
The artist's in the States and no one else can work the switch.'
He won the krillion dollar Kevin Dennis Art Award
For an unentitled sculpture called 'Inflatable Surfboard'.
'Isn't my Peter brilliant,' said his model girlfriend Tania;
We all agreed, and smoked, and ate our take-away lasagne.
The wine flowed and the ouzo and the pipe of pot was passed,
And many eyes were moist when Janis Joplin sang full blast;
But, like poor Jim and Janis, cut off before their prime,
The evening's diamond stylus revolved for the last time.
We found our coats upon the bed, most of them suede and
   fringy,
To think (thought I) it once was said that terraces were dingy!
We filed into the Fitzroy night, the time had come to part,
We bade our host a stoned farewell, and envied all his art.

It must have been a week ago I saw young Peter Jason,
Although he had the same moustache, he had a different face
  on!
'I say, old chap, are you OK? Are you still with Tania Ferris?
You've got some great investments in that super little terrace.'
He looked at me with wailing eyes, hot tears began to bubble,
'We only had a lease,' he croaked, 'it's now a pile of rubble.'
'But why?' I gasped, 'with all your cash? I mean, that place
  was vital!'
'I know,' he said, with sobbing head, *'they couldn't trace the
  title[1].'*
  1970

ODE TO THE SKIPPING GIRL¹

for Keith Dunstan

The trams are still pale green and pretty
And the roof of the Shrine has been polished,
But most of the rest of the city
Has either been ruined or demolished
They haven't pulled down Melbourne Grammar
Though they've wrecked every decent old pub,
And the shadow of Whelan's² lead hammer
Hangs over the old Melbourne Club.
Now we've all got a car and a telly
And a fridge full of goodies and liquor,
If we concrete the whole Yarra Valley
We can get to work five minutes quicker!
For though Progress can sometimes be tawdry,
Our town planners are brilliant and clever;
(Though I privately pray little Audrey³
Will outshine them, and skip on forever).

1970

ODE TO THE NEW NINE-BY-FIVE[1]

An inaugural recitation

G   & S on the pianoforte,
The babble of laughter and wine,
Melbourne Bohemia nicely naughty
In 1889.
Stock, Japonica, daffodil,
Cigar lids and cigarette fumes,
Liberty silks from Cullis and Hill
On the walls of Buxton's Rooms.
McCubbin smiling, Streeton merry,
Conder paralytic;
A nice cheroot and a glass of sherry
For Smith, the *Argus* critic.
Smith took a cab through the August vapour,
Sat at his roll-top desk,
Roberts was first to see the paper,
'A pain to the eye . . . grotesque.'

■　　■　　■

Of the artists who painted on cedar board
Not one remains alive,
And only a used-car man can afford
An original 'nine-by-five'.

But a spinster in nineteen fifty-four
Who dwelt in the Yarra Valley
Found some funny old lids at the back of a drawer
Ideal for kindling a 'mallee'.[2]
Cold grey ash in an Ivanhoe grate
Are those poems the artists gave us,
And the hills that enraptured them groan with the weight
Of Jennings and Craig Davis.[3]
Boxes at Box Hill, poor Bulleen,
Bulldozed and desecrated;
Templestowe plundered and obscene,
And Doncaster castrated.
The riverbank Roberts used to roam
Makes a beautiful Shopping Mall,
And why not erect a Prestige Home
With a sling to your Council pal?
Gone are the rooms they held their club in,
Smike and Bulldog and K,[4]
Richardson and Prof McCubbin,
Long ago — far away.
Lopped are those Heidelberg orchard twigs
Where the spring of our art unfurled,
While Sir Henry Bolte[5] proudly digs
A quarry for the world.

ENVOI
It seemed a fitting and a nice idea
To invite this company assembled here,

And see how diverse artists might contrive
To fit their genius to the nine-by-five.
A charming exercise, a test of skill,
An act of homage? Call it what you will.
Just as the oak from tiny acorn stems,
Likewise the cedar yields these painted gems;
For, in this ponderous age, it's sweet to wander
Down cedar'd paths with Streeton, Roberts, Conder.
And so, in honour of the things they did
We gather here tonight, and dips our lid.[6]

1971

ODE TO THE QUEEN VICTORIA BUILDING, SYDNEY

Written when it was threatened by demolition in 1971

Your domes dream of Constantinople,
Façade picturesque;
Stained glass that once glowed like an opal,
Sydney Romanesque.

They built you way back in the Boom Time,
The Opulent Era;
But now in the seventies' Doom Time
The Wrecker steals nearer.

The noose of Progress slowly throttles
The old and the brave;
New towers rise like giant jumbo bottles
Of cheap aftershave.

How we hate all that sandstone as golden
As obsolete guineas;
With nowhere to stable our Holden
Or tether our Minis.

A casino, car park or urinal
Would grace such a site,
The end could be painless and final,
The deed done by night.[1]

Reactionary ratbags won't budge us
Nor sentiment sway;
But how will Posterity judge us
Ten years from today?

1971

WATTLE PARK BLUES

Back in the wattled thirties
Before the world went dark,
They built this noble chalet
On the crest of Wattle Park.
The trammies on their days off
Came for Devonshire teas,
And outside the kiddies seesawed
With mercurochromy knees[1].
A graveyard for old cable trams
Lay below us in the valley,
Where we played till creamy soda time
And dixies[2] in the chalet.
How we envied the conductor
On the tram on which we'd come.
With his cubes of coloured tickets,
Nippled rubber on his thumb.
Loved his uniform of navy serge,
Scarlet piping on lapel;
Wished we could say, *Move down the car,*
And tug that leather bell.
Above us in the giant gums
Were bird houses built on high,
Little chalets for the maggies,
Tudor suburbs in the sky.

■ ■ ■

We grew older, came less often,
To watch the wattles burst here,
Though Geoff, Jeanette and Alison
Each had their twenty-firsts here;
But we'd outgrown creamy sodas,
Were spottier — and thirstier.
We drank Pimms and puffed on Garricks,
Hugged gardenia'd girlfriends hard,
As we parked our mothers' cars by night
Along the Boulevard,
And Wattle Park was quite forgotten
And the trams' metallic rumble.
Dear to the heart of childhood,
Like the taste of Violet Crumble.
And so dear friends and strangers
I presume to be your guide
To the terminus of memory
I have shouted[3] you a ride.
To the place where me and Colin
And a thousand kiddies more
Picnicked underneath the pollen
In the days before the War.
Today the trees seem sparser
The old cable trams have gone,
But they still serve in the chalet
Melbourne's finest buttered scone.

1974

26

ODE TO THE MELBOURNE THEATRE COMPANY[1]

for Zoe Caldwell

Back in the early fifties in the Age of Brick Veneer
The theatre in Melbourne had an olde worlde atmosphere;
The lights of Exhibition Street twinkled their cosy welcome
And matinees all smelt like church — of hats and gloves and
 talcum.
Here flocked the fans of Glad and Max, Madge Elliott and
 Cyril,[2]
And chorus boys sang lustily pretending to be virile.
Special occasions lured us there from school or home or
 nursery:
A birthday celebration or a wedding anniversary.
A gardenia, a hired car, a meal at Mario.
And then that big night of the year — a flesh-and-blood live
 show!
With a yard of Hilliers[3] on your lap and our programme we'd
 be certain
Of lots of things to drop and flap from overture to curtain.
Maid of the Mountains, *White Horse Inn*, perhaps *The Desert
 Song*,
Brave artistes sacrificed before that rustling gobbling throng.
But at raffish Middle Park, if your mind was not too narrow,

You could see the wicked Mr Thring[4] at a theatre called The
    Arrow.
Here were performed the latest works of playwrights brave
    and brittle —
Though many preferred a family show at The National or The
    Little.
From such a cultural ferment it's not surprising I suppose
That another Melbourne theatre unobtrusively arose:
The Union Rep came into being — yet no one could foresee
It would become that famous troupe we called the MTC.
The names of those who launched her shows can never be
    forgot:
Zoe Caldwell, Carmel Dunn, Brian Edwards, Alex Scott.
What thespian thrills we since have had!
To what first nights we've been privvy!
Yes, Sumner's[5] stern and thoughtful brow gleams still above
    his skivvy.
For plays to help us think and feel John scours the whole
    world over,
The same old flair, the same old zeal — perhaps the same
    pullover!

When told how old this company was, I scarcely could believe
    it,
For it only seems like yesterday that I was asked to leave it.
I couldn't learn my lines, you see, which wouldn't do at all,
So I was driven to a sordid life in the sleazy music hall.

Since those far days the wound has healed, I've learned to
weigh all factors;
Although I but a comic be, I don't envy real actors.
Of bitter dregs I've drunk enough; of fame I've sipped the
cup,
They still have lines to learn by heart, I have to make them
up.
1980

ODE TO THE MELBOURNE GRAMMAR SCHOOL

for Michael Ball

In the triangle St Kilda Road describes with the Domain
Is a bluestone pile the like of which will not be built again.
It is well that this erection was raised up a mile from town
Or the Melbourne City Council would long since have torn it
    down.
For it is music to a Melbourne ear when old buildings crash
    and fall
And a famous Mr Whelan, who has only got one ball,
Loves nothing more than bouncing it against a bluestone wall.

The masonry of which I speak, where old and new are
    blended
Is of course the Melbourne Grammar School, which most of
    us attended,
And it seems to me appropriate and very meet and right
That we should gather here with gratitude in Moonee Ponds
    tonight.
The Old Tie stands for something and people can be cruel,
If some of us are none too bright or just the average fool,
But they sympathise at once when they learn where we went
    to school.

Remember Bully Taylor's classroom? Desks deep furrowed
and engraved,
And carbolic-scented boarders, half-neglected, half-depraved.
The swarming quad, the Physics lab, which smelt of hard-
boiled eggs,
A visit to the library to view Miss Elliot's legs.
Then Assembly where some fainted or else vaguely lost
control
As we sang a rousing ditty begging with our heart and soul
That something called a Dark Blue Twenty would please make
the leather roll.

And remember all that navy blue from Ball & Welsh and Myer
Filling up St Peter's Chapel from the west door to the choir.
Then in tattered gowns two masters faced the altar with a
lurch —
One bowed, the other didn't, rather proud to be Low
Church.
Hear the strangled Chaplain yodel the last words of the Creed,
Inhale a scent of morning Brylcreem, count how long since
last you peed.
Sing, 'I Vow to Thee My Country'; at the organ, Albert
Greed.

Two afternoons a week were wasted on compulsory sport,
And if you dared dodge a turnout, the game was up if you
were caught.
The prefects loved to exercise their biceps with a cane,
They even boasted muscles where lesser mortals had a brain.

I still see you grey-haired athletes with tracksuits and running
    shoes on,
Puffing along the Boulevard pursuing youth's illusion,
And the trophy which awaits you is called Coronary
    Occlusion.

Where are they now, the prefects, stripped of their awesome
    powers,
Do they miss their footy comrades and the Lifebuoy-scented
    showers?
Do they long to cane a slacker or humiliate a shirk
As they Volvo down to Portsea leaving Helen with the Merc?
They don't miss English Literature or Algebra or sums,
But as middle age envelopes them a poignant feeling comes,
When with thumping heart they recollect those tight blue
    schoolboy bums.

My first glimpse of the Head's study I can vividly recall:
Early wisteria out the window, late Streeton on the wall.
The boss irradiated a stern New Zealand aura,
Intimidating those who failed at Ora or Labora.[1]
It was my lack of sporting prowess that brought me before the
    Head,
He'd heard about artistic talent and he knew where those
    things led.
'I hope you don't turn pansy,' was the first thing that he said.

Then dawned the age of acne and the dances and the parties,
And the girls with bouncing pageboys puffing Garricks with
    the hearties.

There was Alison from Merton Hall, Beverly from Clyde,
And Wendy who left Lauriston too soon to be a bride.
A few years later it was Darling Street, Powerhouse and
Ormond Hall
And the cars parked at Point Ormond where the deepest
shadows fall,
And strains of Dennis Farrington[2] played sweetly through it all.

There are things that bring back memories, returning with a
rush,
Like the scent of squashed gardenias, when the band played
Honey Hush,
And the boys who left the year before coming back to school
to gloat
In new uniform of porkpie hat and double-vented coat.
With their Henry Buck's regalia they were Australia's shining
hopes,
Thrashing MGs down to Portsea, drinking *Glühwein* on the
slopes,
Working in the old man's business; nice uncomplicated dopes.

What committees is your wife on? Are you waiting for a
gong?
Would life have been a little richer if they'd sent you to
Geelong?
Is the chap you're dining opposite the person he appears?
Strange to think you've not set eyes on him for thirty-seven
years!

It could be any night at Glo Glo's, or at Maxims or the Flo;
You see a face across the restaurant that you feel you ought to
    know.
Should you smile or look right past him: was he friend or was
    he foe?

As we sup within the bosom of Moonee's gladdy-mantled
    hills,
Hear those distant shuffling footsteps, feel a wind that slightly
    chills.
For a host of guests unbidden have arrived to share our toasts,
A thousand skeletons with old school ties, *Melbourne Grammar
    ghosts*!
So let's drink to all within the call of good St Peter's bell,
'Life was not meant to be easy', I have heard an old boy tell.[3]
Honour ye the Old School story, let's all keep on doing well.

1981

JUBILEE BLUES[1]

Ungracious stanzas from the guest of honour

No taxis due to rain and I was late,
Not only late but recently turned fifty.
Yet *Quadrant* felt this feat deserved a fête
The night before they re-elected Nifty[2].

I got there damp and infinitely flattered.
The function room was full of *jeu d'esprit*,
And some were there whose friendship really mattered —
Two or three.

Later amidst the camembert and mirth
The dreaded hour arrived to make a speech;
(Chill memories of an audience in Perth
Who wondered if I'd meant to jest or preach.)

A few sought *bons mots* sage and mystical,
Another canvassed Edna on 'the trousseau'.
To speak about oneself seemed egotistical —
Irrelevant, however, not to do so.

Accepting all those warm congratulations
On having fifty years ago been born,
I thought about the manifold frustrations
Of those who make a livelihood of scorn.

Drag howling Caliban to his reflection,
But remember as you show the fool his folly
Your bugbear could well win the next election
In this the land of Tony, Bert and Molly[3].

1984

A Prologue to the Fifties[1]

There is no time warp deeper, gulf more vast
Than that between us and the recent past.
Today, the fifties seems a distant era,
Though in Tasmania it must seem much nearer.
A period of uneventful calm
Too close for comfort — void of period charm.
The Politics of Niceness: clean and staid
That was Australia in the fifth decade.
Before the hairy sixties unleashed sex,
The fifties was the Age of Laminex.
When Melbourne hosted the Olympic Games
When couples called their kiddies fifties' names;
Karen and Bronwyn, Wayne and Craig and Cheryl,
This was the world of Sandy Stone and Beryl.
A period when every housewife's goal
Was to possess a new Fler salad bowl.
The shows were *South Pacific, Paint Your Wagon,*
The claret gurgled from a Wynvale flagon,
Espresso coffee and the ballpoint pen,
The FJ Holden and Old Spice for men.
The rage for square dancing, the new kool mints,
The first ducks up the wall, the Van Gogh prints;
Metal venetians, ballerina lamps,

The birth of TV and those boring stamps.
The Little Patties and the John O'Keefes[2]
Ashtrays with Aboriginal motifs.
Those fifties hues the sixties were to scorn —
Lemon and aqua, burgundy and fawn.
Then came that moment verging on the holy
When white Australians discovered . . . *ravioli!*
Diluted with a little local vino,
Washed down with a big brown-flecked cappuccino.
Nice girls with chignons and Braemar twin sets
Puffed at those Rothmans king-sized cigarettes.
And for sophisticated fifties girls,
Cocktail Sobranies and Barossa pearls,
We had no need for heady cultural frenzies —
We had Ken Rosewall and Sir Robert Menzies.

■ ■ ■

The sixties came — the fifties began to fade
Soon we forgot the Innocent Decade.
A different beat throbbed on those radiograms,
The theatres vanished first, and then the trams.
Developers from Hungary knew no rest
Till Sydney looked like post-war Budapest.
At Bennelong arose a Danish folly,[3]
Highbrow alternative to Bob and Dolly.
. . . Now fashion moves so fast the latest fads
Die sooner than Dame Edna's far-flung glads.
The novelties of a year or two ago

Are now as stale as last week's Iced Vo-Vo.
Jacuzzis, atriums, nouvelle cuisine,
As dated as a Galleon fire screen.
It's hard to know what's retro and what's neo —
Without a reassuring nod from Leo[4].
Tonight a fifties paean I intone,
The life of Alexander Horace Stone.
So join me as I gently excavate
His tomb, Glen Iris, 1958.

1990

AFTER THE EVENT

for Stephen Spender

Remembering a far-off fifties day
You gave us all a talk at Melbourne Uni
Your books were thirteen thousand miles away
From that bleak campus by the Ponds of Moonee.

Alone in the vast lecture hall you stood,
A Poet braving a tall cliff of faces
I bet you wished you were in St John's Wood
Instead of putting hecklers in their places.

Since then, I've talked to students so I know
The need to win; I also know the fear.
I wonder would it help us through the show
If someone in the audience yelled: *I'm here!*
You're doing fine, you'll knock them all for six,
Just sock it to those smug provincial pricks!

Instead I grinned and shuffled with the rest;
When you read *Pylons*, almost cried *Encore!*
It's just as well that neither of us guessed
That in that mob there skulked a son-in-law.

1991

JOURNO

for Clive James

Jealous little journo
In your Balmain[1] hutch
What is it you earn-o?
It can't be very much.
Do you wake up in a cold sweat
And feel you've missed the boat?
Why does every generous epithet
Stick in your bearded throat?

Was it novelist or playwright
That once you longed to be?
Was your rock opera nearly finished
When they axed your subsidy?
It's so long ago the year you scored
All those juicy plums
When Don sat on the Lit Board
Swinging favours to his chums.

Now what is it you always boast
When you hear a famous name?
You could have left him at the post
If you'd played the PR game,

But you're not the type to sell out
Like some Chardonnay Socialist
So instead you beat the hell out
Of Karen when you're pissed

Jealous little journo
Typewriter for hire
Why is it you burn-o,
What consumes you like a fire?
What is it in the whole world
Gives you most distress?
Nearly tears your small green heart out?
'Success' you spit, *'success'*.

1991

THRENODY FOR PATRICK WHITE

for Geoffrey Dutton

In a Federation bungalow beside Centennial Park,
With its joggers in the daytime, perves and muggers after dark,
Lived a famous author hostesses pretend that they have read;
A querulous curmudgeon with a tea-cosy on his head.

He had a vulnerable hauteur, he was arrogant and shy
He had the visage of a dowager with a beady light blue eye,
He wrote at least two masterpieces, his correspondence flowed
    in torrents
With Firbank in one pocket, in the other D. H. Lawrence.

He was generous to young artists; often petty, never mean,
He was a typical high-minded, interbellum, stage-struck
    queen.
Before the War he would have queued to hear Bea Lillie[1] sing,
One imagined him in private dragging up like Douggie Byng[2].

He had a few friends (mostly female), whom he wrote to all
    their lives,
And he loved his male friends too until they traded in their
    wives.

Then he cut them and he dropped them and defamed them
    on the page
You felt he'd once been dropped so cruelly he had to share
    the pain and rage.

He dropped Sid and Geoff and Lawrence, he dropped Bruce
    and Brett and me
He preferred those lisping toadies who wouldn't dare to
    disagree.
With lickspittles round his table he was the Venerated Crank
But the malady was in his bones and he shrank and shrank and
    shrank . . .

Now his writing light is switched off, though his wall-eyed
    dogs still bark
In that Federation garden beside Centennial Park,
Home of the family picnic and the jogger and the mugger;
Oh I pray God doesn't drop *you*, you miserable old bugger.

1991

TYCOONS

You seemed so bright above us
Floating like balloons
And we felt you'd always be there
Our very own tycoons.

Australia seemed to come of age
When you sailed into view
We had Triad slayings, child abuse,
One oil slick – and *you!*

How we loved your daughters' weddings
Grudged you not your yachts and villas
All we lacked to join the Big League
Were race riots and serial killers.

So what went wrong? Where have you vanished?
We've taken it quite hard
For it seems you've all been banished
To the slammer or Gstaad.

Yet in your heyday you were heroes
Like glittering trophied warriors;
Where now are your Fred Williams
And your Whiteleys and your Storriers?[1]

At the Melbourne Cup your marquees
Were like temples to a layman,

Now they've repossessed your car keys
And your lovely boats off Hayman[2].

Why did it set, your lucky star?
At the crunch where was your saviour?
You're exiled now to Harry's bar
Or jogging in Belgravia.

It's the old tall poppy syndrome
And the Media which impugns
The daring and the courage
Of our very own tycoons.

Can you forgive us? Do you miss us?
Is your homeland quite forgot?
Might you come back on a visit
When things here aren't quite so hot?

For we miss *you* – miss you badly
Time heals wounds and time forgets,
As all Australia, proudly, *gladly*
Pays the interest on your debts.

1991

THE SONGS OF

BARRY McKENZIE

THE OLD PACIFIC SEA

for Martin Sharp

AIR: MAGGIE MAY

Oh, I was down by Manly pier
Drinking tubes of ice-cold beer,
With a bucket full of prawns upon me knee;
But when I'd swallowed the last prawn
I had a technicolour yawn,
And I chundered in the old Pacific Sea.

> *CHORUS*
> Drink it up, drink it up,
> Crack another dozen tubes and prawns with me.
> If you want to throw your voice
> Mate, you won't have any choice,
> But to chunder in the old Pacific Sea.

I was sitting in the surf
When a mate of mine called Murph
Asked if he could crack a tube or two with me.
The bastard barely swallowed it
When he went for the big spit,
And he chundered in the old Pacific Sea.

(CHORUS)

There's a lot of ways that you can
Have a ball when you are pukin',
And the secret of it is variety
You can either park a Tiger
From the summit of the Eiger,
Or chunder in the old Pacific Sea.

(Chorus)

I've had liquid laughs in bars
And I've hurled from moving cars,
And I've chuckled when and where it suited me.
But, if I could choose a spot
To regurgitate me lot,
Then I'd chunder in the old Pacific Sea.

> *Chorus*
> Drink it up, drink it up,
> Crack another dozen tubes and prawns with me.
> Why kneel there all alone
> By the big white telephone
> When you can chunder in the old Pacific Sea.

1964

EARL'S COURT BLUES[1]

for Nicholas Garland

Before I left Australia to travel o'er the sea,
I went into our loungeroom and sat on my old father's knee —
He'd spent years in the Outback, in that land of thirst and
   drouth,
And he said to me, 'Son, don't ever look a gift horse in the
   mouth.
If a fella offers you a drink, don't pause to count the cost,
And the same applies to sheilas — *he who hesitates is lost.*'

Well, now I'm in the Old Country and living in Earl's Court[2],
And if you offered me a beer I'd say, 'I'll be in that one sport.'
And the same applies to sheilas, if they're pretty or they're not:
If a girl gives me the old green light, I'm in there like a shot.

    CHORUS
    Oh, I wouldn't say no to an ice-cold beer
    And I wouldn't say no to a naughty,
    Though there ain't much of either over here,
    In a bedsitter in Earl's Court-ee —
    The beer over here isn't fit to drink
    And the sheilas are cold and haughty —
    So, I wouldn't say no to an ice-cold beer
    And I wouldn't say no to a naughty.

Last Saturday me mates and me decided to get tight³,
And I tried to feel up a Pommy sheila later on that night.
When I pinched her behind, she said, 'Do you mind?'
And gave her head a toss.
So I told this Pom, 'Where I come from
The girls all come across!'

(CHORUS)

One day I strode up the Earl's Court Road,
And into a pub I was lured —
'Where do you come from?' said a nosy Pom
As I downed the amber fluid.
So I told him straight, 'I'm Australian mate,
And feel like getting plastered.
But the beer's crook and the girls all look
Like *you*, you Pommy bastard!'

(CHORUS)

I met a tart the other night, and she said, 'Pleased to meet yer.'
So I smiled and said, with a jerk of me head,
'Well, how's about a feature?'⁴
As we drank ice-cold and I got more bold, she took a pack of
     fags out.
And said, 'Let's drink beer, I'm sorry dear,
But tonight I've got the flags out.'

(CHORUS)
1965

THE BALLAD OF THE ONE-EYED TROUSER SNAKE

I've got a little creature,
I suppose you'd say a pet;
And if there's something wrong with him
I don't have to call the vet.
He goes everywhere that I go,
Whether sleeping or awake,
God help me if I ever lost
Me little one-eyed trouser snake.

One day I got to reading
In an old sky pilot's book
About two starkers bastards
Who made the Lord go crook.
They reckoned it was a serpent
That made Eve the apple take,
Cripes, that was no flamin' serpent —
'Twas Adam's one-eyed trouser snake.

I met an arty sheila
I'd never met before,
And something kind of told me
She banged like a shit-house door.

I said, 'Come up and see my etching,'
She said, 'I hope it's not a fake.'
I said, 'The only thing that's etchin
Is me one-eyed trouser snake.'

1972

IF IT WAS RAINING VIRGINS

for Peter Cook

I wouldn't win a kick in a riot,
I always seem to cop the lousy luck.
And when I'm with a bird, I always try it —
But they brush me off like they was Lady Muck.
Oh, the happiness I seek
Has vanished up shit creek . . .

> CHORUS
> If it was raining virgins,
> I'd be washed down the gutter with a poof.
> When I feel me heart-throbs surgin',
> The sheilas just tell me to bugger off!
> Love seems to shoot through when I want it to stay —
> I'm as lonely as a bastard on Father's Day.
> If it was raining virgins,
> I'd be washed down the gutter with a poof.

I wouldn't win a poke in a fire.
In the Mallee I'd be stuffed to find a root.
When I touch a sheila's knee and move it higher,
My bollocks come in contact with her boot.
The only girl I seem to charm
Is me old mate, Mrs Palm . . .

Some sheilas are supposed to be cinches,
But they never seem to cop my virile powers.
And it isn't that I'm all that many inches
Short of Casanovas I've seen in the showers.
Where is the girl who'll beg and screech
To squeeze me blackheads on the beach?

> *CHORUS*
> Oh, if it was raining virgins,
> I'd be washed down the gutter with a poof.
> When I feel me heart-throb surgin',
> The sheilas just tell me to bugger off!
> Love seems to shoot through, when I say *wait a tick!*
> At the knock shop wedding, I'm the spare prick.
> Oh, if it was raining virgins,
> I'd be washed down the gutter with a poof.

1972

AUSTRALIAN REPARTEE[1]

for Bruce Beresford

Australians are noted for their wit
We're famed for our repartee,
And when we meet a stuck-up Brit
We give him a sample free.
When a whingeing Pommy comes the raw prawn
And gives our ears a bash,
We turn on him a look of scorn
And we tell him quick as a flash.

> CHORUS
> Oh, I hope all yer chooks turn to Emus
> Kick yer dunny down flat to the grass.
> I hope yer balls turn to bicycle wheels
> And back-pedal up yer arse.
> I hope every lah de dah Pommy like you
> Gets the trots when he swallows the plum.
> Go and dip yer left eye in hot cocky shit
> And stick yer head up a dead bear's bum.

One day I met a migrant Pom
And bought the poor cow a drink.
From the way the bastard was carrying on
You'd reckon his shit didn't stink.

I kept me head till this poofter said
The Brits could lick us at cricket.
Then I showed him the rough end of a pineapple
And I told him where he could stick it.
I said . . .

(CHORUS)

Now Australian's power of eloquence
Is part of our national glory.
You just have to listen to Parliament
To cop our oratory.
Our politician's wit is quick
His voice is rich in timbre★.
So one of these days, I won't be amazed
To hear *this* speech in Canberra★★.

> CHORUS (VARIANT AT END)
> Oh, I hope all yer chooks turn to Emus
> Kick yer dunny down flat to the grass.
> I hope yer balls turn to bicycle wheels
> And back-pedal up yer arse.
> I hope the Right Honourable Member
> Will permit me to give him the drum.
> Go and dip your left eye etc . . .

★ *pronounced tam-bra*
★★ *pronounced Can-bra*
1972

THE LAYS OF ◼

LES PATTERSON

UNSUITABLE FOR WOMEN-FOLK

THE YARTZ[1]

for Ian Davidson

W hat is it I like more than tarts?
The Yartz.
What passes through my mind in fits and starts?
You've guessed,
The Yartz.
Wherever you may roam in foreign parts,
Australia always seems to top the charts
Re in terms of[2]
The Yartz.
What have we got these great artistic skills for
That other lands would gladly give their pills for?
Here's hoping the Government will find the means for
Supporting what all Aussies cream their jeans for:
Fillums and opera, macramé work and pomes,
Hectares and tonnes of culture in all homes.
This isn't just a dream — it's come to pass,
If you don't believe me kiss my arse.

1975

THE WORKAHOLIC

A question that's on really everyone's mind,
Is how does a person like me unwind?
Do I listen to Debussy symphonies,
Or do yoga positions down on my knees?

Whenever I'm tired, run down and uptight,
My hardy organism flashes me the red light.
I front up at a clinic in refined Adelaide,
Where a physiotherapist comes to my aid.
She's a fully trained lass who understands,
And I shove all my worries in her capable hands.

1978

SONNET OF CIVIC PRIDE

I love our Australian cities,
I'm one of the few that cares,
And I'm looking for way-out statues
To bung in our city squares.

I will not cease from mortal strife,
Nor will the taxpayer's money sleep in my hand,
Till I have built a viable sociologically unitised urban ecosphere
In Australia's brown unpleasant land.

1978

FITNESS

I go jogging once a week
I suppose you'd call me a fitness freak.

The wife and me have got single beds,
Cos my jogging rips the sheets to shreds.

1978

THE MEDIA

Of no item is our culture needier,
Than the Media.
Yet of talent there is nothing greedier,
Than the bloody Media.
It's choc-a-block with info like an encyclopaedia,
That's the Media!

Overseas types have frankly been amazed
When on our local TV they have gazed.
I've never in my life seen foreign eyes grow beadier
Than when they've copped an eyeful of the Australian Media.

1978

THE BALLAD OF LES THE KNIFE

With no apologies to Bert Brecht

You'll be a family favourite, that's a cert,
If you sing your kiddies a ditty by Bert.
To remember 'em you'd need a memory like an elephant's,
But what they lack in tune they gain in relevance.

1978

LES AT LEISURE

Despite my up-market élitist veneer,
I like an informal relaxed atmosphere.
And there's nowhere more peaceful — say what you might —
Than the leisurely pace of an Aussie building site.

1978

Burying the Hatchet

I like to hang out with delegations of Japs,
And they're never happier than when they're taking snaps.
But forgot are the days when these blokes used to fight us,
I just think of them now as Aussie dwarves with hepatitis.

1978

Objets d'Abo

Tasmanian abo's are thin on the ground,
But their beautiful artefacts seem to abound.
Ripping them off in Taiwan has become quite a racket,
But these originals on velvet in my own private collection
Are worth a bloody packet.

1978

ODE TO CONSERVATION[1]

The most meaningful quid you ever spent
Would *have* to be on the environment.
The Russians are a pretty gloomy lot,
But there's one ripper idea they've got.
Their hearts must be generous and big
Cos they care where *other* countries dig!
It puts the Commos in a rage
If we spoil our bushland heritage
By digging for uranium and other muck
Just to win a foreign buck.
I'm not a Commo but my favourite hobby
Is fart-arsing around the environment lobby.
And I *may* owe our comrades a little apology
But would *they* mind if we helped them with *their* ecology?

1978

MIDDAY MUSINGS

I'm wearing my casting director's hat
And backing a Patterson hunch,
Kicking a few ideas around
At a typical working lunch.

From where I sit her parameters
Look pretty up-front to me,
And if my homework is correct
We'll be in the motel by three.

1978

MY ROOTS

I'm a terribly private person
And I keep my profile low,
Though there's millions of intimate questions
The Media's busting to know.
But when they quiz me about my family life
I suddenly come on vague,
Cos it isn't fair for publicity's glare
To strike Gwennie and Karen and Craig.

As if life isn't difficult enough
For Australia's governing class
Without some nosy journo trying to stuff
A camera up your wife's arse.

Though the sheilas are after my body,
I'm loyal to the soles of my boots.
I always come home again
To Craig, Karen and Gwen —
For a man needs his occasional roots.

1978

69

PATTERSON'S PRAYER

for Edward Clark

There's nothing I would rather be
Than Chairman of the ABC.

1978

MADAME TOSSHARD'S WAXWORKS[1]

for Rosamund Freeman-Attwood

I stand here before my old media buddies
As Dean of the School of Australian Studies[2],
And it's as an ACADEMIC I come
To praise MADAME TOSSHARD, my artistic old chum.
Once she guided me round this historical show
And said, 'Any suggestions, Les, just let me know.
We've got Royals and ratbags, the humble and noble.
There's just one prerequisite — their fame must be global.'
So I told Madame Tosshard, 'What your lovely show lacks
Is a FAMOUS AUSTRALIAN made out of wax.'
Then without me prompting, old Madame T
Said, 'Let's approach Dame Edna on bended knee.
She's the only Aussie who's loved and adored
By all races and creeds across the board.
But Edna's so glamorous and stunning
She could even elude our technicians' cunning!'

Well, they went to her shows,
Read her best-selling books,
Shoved a tape measure into her intimate nooks;
They copied her hair style down to the last lock.
Some nuns nearly went blind stitching jewels on her frock.

Madame Tosshard said, 'Les, your dream has come true —
We've immortalised Edna, and the *next one is you!*
I'd like to hand-mould your features in private one day
With a big lump of something that won't melt away.'
But until Madame Tosshard turns her hand to me
I'll flash something at you that you're bursting to see.
For now it's with pleasure that I unveil yer
Woman of wax — *Queen of Australia.*
From the tip of your glad to the jewels on yer glasses,
You've proved Australians have culture right up to our arses.

1979

HOME IS WHERE THE YARTZ IS

Our ancient bush
and mountain peaks
never swarmed
with Gyppos
and Greeks.
That's the reason why
we're up
the creek
when it comes to unearthing
the odd
antique.
If you dug under Sydney,
Melbourne
and Perth,
all you'd find
is a dirty great load
of earth.

The statue I like
in our local museum
shows a starkers young sheila
as rarely you see 'em.
I don't know the pyramid

she came from,
but I'd reckon she'd have to be worth
a bomb.
Archaeologists
will dig her up one day
under hectares of crap and clay.
When you and me are quite forgot
they'll say, 'The Yartz
in Australia
must've been shit hot!'

1981

CAMBRIDGE COUPLETS[1]

Tonight you have donned your most solemn regalia
To extol the glory of my homeland, Australia;
And I, humble son of that continent brown,
Proudly accept this cap and gown.

But what does the average bloke expect
When he visits this shrine of intellect?
A bunch of poofters and Brideshead[2] blighters,
Shirt-lifters and Pommy pillow-biters?
The girls love my laid-back Australian style
When I walk past they flash me the vertical smile,
They'd all love to join me in a Cambridge punt
For a seminar on Immanuel Kant.
But you're a bonzer bunch of lasses and lads,
And I'm real proud to be honoured by youse undergrads.
So, no matter what any smart bastard sez:
When you think of Australia please think of old Les;
And with that, gentle ladies, may I now withdraw,
And I haven't said *that* to a woman before!

1981

ODE TO PARKY[1]

There's a bloke who's keenly watched and widely read,
Who always hits the nail on the head.
He kicked off modestly in the UK
And he's a world celebrity today.

If he gets nervous, well, it's never showed —
His face is like a mile of rugged road,
His crow's feet are the dried-up beds of smiles
And his best friends are aware that he's got piles
— Of charm, pizzazz and British spunk and phlegm;
Of TV interviewers he's the gem.
He could interview a Zulu or Iraqi
and make it interesting;
His name is Parky.

This bloke can conjure laughter and applause
In the wake of Ratbags, Poofs and Crashing Bores.
And if he's pushed for spicy dialogue
He'll ask you if you've ever nudged the grog.

Australian critics are all chippy guys,
They tried to chop old Parky down to size.
Some even said: 'Go back where you come from —
We won't be taught charisma by a Pom.'
But he knows the average Aussie journalist
Is following orders, jealous or half pissed!

He smiles, he does his job, he doesn't care;
When you're the top where do you go from there?
So raise your glass of lager, rum or saki,
Whether you be Hun or Nip or Darkie,
And drink the health of my old cobber — PARKY!

1982

TWO SCORE AND TEN . . .

If you've not heard the news then you'd have to be deaf:
Barry Humphries next Friday attains the big F.
But F doesn't just stand for the two score and ten
It means a lot more to red-blooded men.
For F stands for FACULTIES we don't mind if we lose,
So long as it's in a good cause like the BOOZE.
And F stands for the FEATURES that make Australia so
   beaut,
Like FUNNEL-WEB spiders and FANNIES and FRUIT;
FAST-BOWLERS like Dennis, and yacht race FIRST
   PRIZES,
And F stands for FUN BAGS in popular sizes.
F's for our FILLUMS that get better and better —
I reckon F is Australia's most often used letter.
It's the FAST FLAMIN' FORTUNE each true Aussie seeks
With the dirty work all done by Boat People and Greeks.
Lastly F stands for FOSTERS — just one of the beverages
We bring up on birthdays like Dame Edna Everage's!

1984

ODE TO THE MERLIN COMPLEX[1]

If I asked you to name the nicest town on earth,
You wouldn't be far wrong if you said Perth.
My luxury suite would woo the most resistant,
Boy, did it work with my research assistant!
The nicest place to entertain a girl in
Just has to be this luxury Hotel Merlin.
Gorgeous soft carpets,
Dirty great big rooms,
Lovely fresh air
And no pollution fumes.
Well-trained sheilas on the switchboard too,
Who if your wife calls *never put her through*.
For if a man is halfway through dictation
A phone call could cause a sticky situation.
The food in all the restaurants is perfection,
And the dunnies are sanitised for your protection.

I live in pubs so I know all the ropes,
If you can't knock off the maids knock off the soaps.
For Perth's a town young architects get rich in;
It sure beats tarting up some dickhead's kitchen.[2]

This is the best joint in which I've stayed,
And the blokes who built it deserve an accolade.
So before the final drinks they serve,
Give 'em the clap they all richly deserve.

1984

ODE TO CAIRNS[1]

There's a haven in Australia where I always like to go
When the time arrives to make vacation plans;
And in case you were in doubt the place I let it all hang out
Is far north Queensland, and the city is called Cairns★.

It was a friend of my wife Gwen's who first put me on to
    Cairns★★,
She was an usherette with a very lovely smile.
She once said, 'Pleased to meetcha' just before the double
    feature,
And after that she steered me firmly up the aisle.

At the time of which I speak, my manhood was at its peak,
And the sheilas used to swoon in disbelief.
I used to bring my female friends for raunchy tropical weekends
To this paradise beside the Barrier Reef.

Well, to cut a long one short, I always had a rort,
And the taxpayer — God bless you — paid the cheque.
But my romantic escapades are memories that fade
As quickly as the lovebites on my neck.

It's a diplomat's delight to catch a Queensland flight
And escape the world of work and strife and marriage;
But the climax of the trip is to gaze down at the strip
And know the time has come to drop your undercarriage.

I've developed quite a terror of all that snooping in Canberra
And them allegations made without foundation.
I'd rather lie beneath the palms, research assistant in me arms
And know the bastards haven't taped me conversation.

Now, you know north Queensland's there, race your loved
    ones off by air
For a holiday you'll cherish all your life.
It's such a ripper little spot that this time, I kid you not:
I weakened — and *nearly* brought the wife.

* *pronounced Kanz*
** *pronouned Kenz*
        1984

IN TERMS OF MY NATURAL LIFE[1]

I am an Australian in terms of Nation
And a public servant in terms of vocation,
But there's one thing amazes my critics and that's
How many I wear in terms of hats.
I chair the Cheese Board, I front the Yartz;
You could term me a man of many parts.
I'm a Renaissance type, if you know the term,
And I've held long office in terms of term.
Yes, I've long served Australia in terms of years
And in terms of refreshment I like a few beers.
My opponents are mongrels, scum and worms
Who I bucket in no uncertain terms;
And my rich vocabulary always features
Large in terms of my public speeches.
My favourite terms in terms of debate
Are: 'broad-based package' and 'orchestrate'.
But one term I never employ is 'failure',
Especially when talking in terms of Australia!
For in terms of lifestyle we've got the germs of
A ripper concept to think in terms of.
Yes, in terms of charisma I've got the game mastered:
In anyone's terms I'm a *well-liked bastard.*

1985

SALUTE TO EDNA[1]

Some people love Australia for its surfing and its sun,
Other people flock here in search of indoor fun.
Our scenery lures some tourists, and our marsupials take the
 prize,
But I guess it's our dirt-cheap dollar gets 'em swarming here
 like flies.
Yet although my own portfolio is tourism, cheese and the
 Yartz,
When they ask me what's world class down under
I tell 'em *Aussie tarts!*
Our womenfolk are legendary, or so history clearly states —
Look at Dame Nellie Melba, Eliza Fraser, Daisy Bates.
There's Judy Davis, Wendy Hughes and little Jackie Weaver,
Each one of them deserves the title: feminine achiever.
Where would Australian Opera be without good old Dame
 Joan?
And when world athletes gasped for breath, Dawn Fraser
 swam alone.
Carla Zampatti, Little Pru and raunchy Jenny Kee
Have made Australian fashion the envy of Paree.
May Gibbs and Col McCullough of *Snugglepot* and *Thornbirds*
 fame
Have both brought credibility to Australian literature's name.
I'm not a bloody chauvinist like other Aussie men,

And I can name more great women, including my wife Gwen.
But there is a wondrous woman that I'd be stupid to ignore,
She's the reason for this TV show that we've all come here
  for.
Tonight she's in the hot seat, and boy is that seat hot —
She's Australia's best-known star by far, the greatest that we've
  got.
One day they'll build her monument in marble, gold and
  bronze,
But meanwhile she's here in the flesh: Edna from Moonee
  Ponds!
  1985

Dr Sir Les Patterson's Press Club Epic[1]

Today I've cut down on my lunchtime beers,
The better to confront you all — my Peers.
I can't pretend I don't enjoy a glass,
But when I have to get up off my arse
And make a speech that's nationwide, I choose
To nudge, less savagely, the La Perouse[2].

Sydney's my birthplace, and they say it shows,
But date of birth I'd rather not disclose.
A lithe young man lurks in this Hong Kong suit
Which men admire and sheilas long to root.
At school I left the other boys for dead
In what I did behind the shelter shed[3],
And though no teacher's pet or sissy swot,
I taught some girls a lesson ne'er forgot.
Sometimes reminders of them distant days
Come back to me in sweet nostalgic ways:
I might be chairing some Yartz Seminar,
And suddenly I see a lady far
To the back, flash me a knowing look,
While I rave on about some play or book.
Who is she? The poor cow should wear a bag —
Frankly she looks like old Don Chipp[4] in drag!

And yet . . . ? A childhood memory slowly dawns:
I gave her one beneath the peppercorns.
It happens to us all, part of life's game —
The sheilas all grow old, *we* stay the same.

Just take my wife, the lovely Lady Gwen.
She could have chosen many other men.
A few had better jobs and handsome faces,
But somehow Gwen knew I was going places.
We married, had two kids, and only then
I started going places . . . *without Gwen*.
She copped it sweet, I didn't get much flak,
For Gwen was never mad about the sack,
And this produced a few domestic dramas:
She once sewed up the fly on my pyjamas!
But in the end I bowed to her regime —
A dry peck on the cheek and a wet dream.
These days if I play 'round I never tell 'er,
Nor come home till the lovebites have turned yeller.
I love that kid a lot to be quite candid,
She's brought up Craig and Karen single-handed.
Soft's not a word applied to me by many,
But I'm an old softie when it comes to Gwennie.
No matter what in anger my wife sez —
She's taught those kiddies to be proud of Les.

Sometimes my thoughts will gravitate to sex.
During some opera show of Janáček's.
Slumped in my penguin gear and slightly dozing,

I watch Dame Joan's[5] gob opening and closing,
While in my mind I hear some sheila pant,
'I'll do it for a Bicentennial grant.'
Last night I went a little bit too far
With one bird in my diplomatic car.
She wanted me to swing her a few Gs
To help some puppet theatre off its knees.
I grogged her up, but in the car she chundered,
So I dropped the little lady home — *unfunded*.
She knocked me back, as certain women can;
I think she could've been an Ombudsman[6].

Today I proudly wear my favourite hat:
Les Patterson — Career Diplomat.
Some wowsers still call me 'King of the Ockers',
But every successful Aussie has his knockers.
Journos have knocked me umpteen times a year;
They're down the tubes — but Patterson's still here!
Sometimes I cop a nasty bit of flak
From some poor old publicity-starved hack.
They reckon they can shaft me with their snide
Suggestions that I'm 'letting down the side'.
I guess if I were some poor clapped-out failure,
I'd finger blokes for rubbishing Australia.
Pig's arse I would! I think I'd sooner cark it[7]
Than sell out to the phoney flag-waving market.
I've worked harder than any man alive
To drag Australia into '85.

We don't want diplomats all smug and smarmy
Flogging our cheeses, fillums and macramé.
Australia needs a leader strong and craggy
Like me, to stick our policies up Maggie.
Though once I helped to groom our leader, Bob,
I doubt I'll cop that little bugger's job.
Yet even in the parliamentary forum
We still keep up this front of false decorum.
And whether we come from Town or from the Mulga,
The epithet we all detest is 'vulgar'.
The world can give us any label bar
The one that tells us what we really are.
We might like snow peas and eat pecan nuts,
But scratch an Aussie and he's rough as guts!
Thank God we *are* like that, but still you find
This hankering to come across 'refined'.
A mirror held to the Australian
Will make us scream like Shakespeare's Caliban.

■   ■   ■

Sometimes I think I might just chuck it all
And hang a few Fred Williams[8] on my wall,
Sip chardonnay grown by some merchant banker
And read the *National Times*[9] like any wanker.
Gwen would be happy, that's a certain fact,
The Press would say, 'Les has cleaned up his act.'
But that's just not the way I like to tick —
Patterson has always been a maverick.

I want to put this country on the map,
Not stay at home looking for backs to slap.
I want Australia to get up and go,
Not be carved up by Cain and Wran and Joh.[10]
Paul Keating's[11] done to our long business lunches
What AIDS has done to all those mattress munchers.
So out with the wowsers and the demagogues
Before this land of ours goes to the dogs.

1985

ODE TO THE SMH GOOD FOOD GUIDE[1]

Oft when I think back to them dark old days,
The restaurant writers had a favourite phrase:
They never *chose* the prawns or garlic bread,
But they, or their companions, 'plumped' instead.
They plumped for the soup, they plumped for cheese and bicks;
They plumped themselves to death the stupid pricks.
But at last we have a gourmet guide that's handy,
In case you're hungry, thirsty or plain randy.
A book that tells you not just where to eat
But where to find Sydney's Guttersnipe Elite.
We've come a long way from the pie and sauce,
With yabbies and snowpeas on every course.
And who'd have thought we'd all so gladly pay
To drink some dickhead lawyer's chardonnay?
This little guide is overflowing, full
Of information, wit — a touch of bull.
I love it — but Les Patterson loves eating,
And stopping me will take more than Paul Keating![2]

1985

ODE TO 'THE BIG COOK BOOK'[1]

Tonight I've had a drink to calm my nerves,
To give this book the send off it deserves.
Let's face it, Australia frankly takes the prize
As the best place on earth to satirise.
Our gutter politics, our second-raters,
Our loud-mouthed bullies and professional haters.
All need the book thrown at them — or the Bible,
But thanks to our draconian laws of libel
The satirist must shut up or cop a writ
From some corrupt and powerful old shit.

It's chaps like Patrick and his colleague, Max[2],
Who, spite of all, continue to make cracks
Against Establishment, with satire deft —
They even sometimes criticise THE LEFT!

I'm deeply honoured to be standing here
To praise this peak in Patrick Cook's career.
For he belongs by talent and by right
To a great heritage in black and white:
Phil May, the Lindsays, Will Dyson and Low,
Banks, Gurney, Mercier, Stan Cross and Co.,
Jim Russell, Rigby, Petty, Sharp and Tanner,
And the great Leunig march 'neath the same banner;

George Sprod and Spooner, Pickering and Moir —
Australia's answers to Lautrec and Goya[3].
A cavalcade of great and gifted men
Who pricked our South Sea bubbles with their pen.
Long may Cook's wit live on the *National*'s[4] page
That we maintain some laughter with our rage.

1985

LES PATTERSON'S POETIC ADDRESS TO THE PRESS[1]

Leslie Patterson is my name
And I welcome you all to old Drury Lane.
We've laid on a drink and a morsel of grub
To lure all youse bastards from your Fleet Street pubs.
I know all too well you need grog on the menu
To entice a journo to a cultural venue.

But I'm here to announce an artistic coup,
And frankly we can't kick it off without you!
We need publicity to rake in the shekels,
But I must draw the line at kissing your freckles.
COLUMN INCHES, my Friends, is the name of the game,
And if this show's a turkey we'll know who's to blame.
This is an occasion your conscience will feel better for,
So whip out your felt tips and let rip with a metaphor.

I happen to hail from a wonderful land
Whose headquarters are situate just down the Strand[2].
And my brief this morning from the moment I rose
Is to plug the best of Dame Edna's shows.
This wonderful sheila, so it appears,
Has been away from the West End Stage for three fuckin' years!
And now she returns without rhyme or reason
To give you Poms a ten-week season.

This actress has come at the height of her power,
Bringing light to England's darkest hour.
So kindly I beg you, good folk, raise thy glass —
This show is a much needed shot in the arse.

Now before you all rush back to your brewers,
A word of advice to theatre reviewers:
Make sure you don't give Dame Edna a stinker,
Or she'll rip off your balls like she's done with Jack Tinker[3].

1986

MY GONG

for Peter Young

People are always asking me, they quiz me loud and long
And the thing the bastards want to know, is how I got my gong.
How come an old Republican, like me to be specific,
Could accept from Betty Britain a Royal fuckin' honorific?
I've copped aggro from my colleagues and a heap of media flak,
So I'm going to spill the beans to get the journos off my back.

When the Queen came to Australia a year or two ago
Prince Philip intimated that he'd like to see a show.
At the time I was the Minister for Abbos and the Yartz.
And I organised a concert that really touched their Royal hearts.
Rolf, Kamahl, and Little Pattie — you should have heard the
    audience cheer,
And a line of ballet dancers with fun-bags out to *here*!
When we had a grog at interval Phil gave me a big smile
'I like you Les,' he said, 'For an Australian you've got style.
I liked your speech tonight as well, do you write all your stuff?'
So I told him modestly my little talk was off the cuff.
'I need you Les,' Phil blurted out, 'my speeches are that boring
I half drop off while making them and I hear the audience
    snoring.
I try to spice them up with odd colloquialisms like 'bloody'
But I need *your* input; how'd you like a hot line to my study?'

All that happened a few years ago and it's worked out pretty
  well.
Though I've supplied the odd one-liner that Prince Philip
  cannot tell.
Like that beaut about the definition of an Irish Jig,
And the one about the darkie, and the parrot and the pig.
So whenever I'm in London I have to sneak into the palace
Cos his official team of speech writers get pretty bloody
  jealous,
They've all been to University and copped some posh degree
So they get pissed off that the Queen's hubby prefers
  anecdotes by me!

Well that's how I scored my Knighthood, and frankly it
  surprised me,
Though I disagree with knockers who say it's compromised
  me,
I'm still well left-of-centre so those taunts can't hurt me much,
And I'm buggered if a title could make Les lose the common
  touch.
Pommy union men cop PEERAGES, and that's a well known
  fact,
And I know a Labor big-wig whose integrity's intact —
The Governor General of Australia is an old friend tried and
  true
He was born and raised in Queensland and people think that I
  was too.

Yonks ago at Yarralumla where we'd both been asked to dine
I seen him give our dear Queen's photo the old two finger
  sign.
But it only took a cuppa and a bickie at Buck House
For Bill to get a taste for Bollinger and caviar and grouse!
Now since he's won the Big Job he's on a strictly champagne
  diet
And they reckon he plays polo and breeds corgis on the quiet.
So here's my advice to Labor men who get honoured by the
  Crown:
Graciously accept the perks but for Christ's Sake play it down
As I whispered to my Sovereign on the day I got my gong:
'When me mates are watching do you mind if I sit down for
  your song?'
        1991

UP THE REPUBLIC
for Clyde Packer

Australia's independence has long been my ambition,
But you wouldn't catch me signing a Republican petition,
Have you seen the types who sign them? What a bunch of
   piss-ants, jeez!
From sentimental pinko novelists to shonky young QCs,
Dramaturges who've long been guzzling at the Yartz Council
   trough,
And grizzled grantees washed up from the golden days of
   Gough;
Rich admen turned to Gurus and jumped-up copywriters,
Armani-suited journos and opera-loving pillow-biters.
Pious pollies who would sell their poor old mothers for a bob;
My oath I'm a Republican — but forgive me, I'm a snob!

                                                    1991

DAME EDNA
▪ EVERAGE ▪

MAROAN[1]

for Elizabeth Jolley

You've read in all the magazines
About the Colour Question:
Should we be black, off-white or beige?
May I make a suggestion:
Maroan's my favourite colour,
It's a lovely shade I think —
It's a real hard colour to describe,
Not purple — and not pink.

All our family loves it and
You ought to see our home,
From the bedroom to the laundry —
Every room's maroan!
When we bought our home in Moonee Ponds
It didn't have a phone,
But it had one thing to offer:
The toilet was maroan.

Look, I fell in love with it at once,
I felt the place was mine.
You see the day I married Norm
My bridesmaids were in wine.
Our wedding cake was iced to match
And glowed in splendour lonely,

And they drank our toast in burgundy
Which sparkled so maroanly.

The day my mother had her turn
We heard an awful groan,
I dropped young Ken, dashed to her room
And there she was — maroan.
And now she's in the twilight home,
We're going to England soon.
But one English custom gets my goat:
They call maroan 'maroon'??

1955

EDNA'S HYMN[1]

Australia is a Saturday
With races on the trannie,
Australia is the talcy smell
Of someone else's granny.
Australia is a kiddie
With zinc cream on his nose,
Australia's voice is Melba's[2] voice,
It's also Normie Rowe's[3].
Australia's famous postage stamps
Are stuffed with flowers and fauna,
Australia is the little man
Who's open round the corner.
Australia is a sunburnt land
Of sand and surf and snow;
All ye who do not love her
Ye know where ye can go.

1968

THE TURNTABLE OF LIFE

Outside in the garden, the rhodies were damp;
Inside was a-shine with a candlewick lamp.
The Galleon fire screen glinted and glowed,
The crumpets were juicy, the jam overflowed.
The mallee-root[1] crumbled to ash in the heat
As we sat holding hands on the Patterson suite.

Oh, those soft winter evenings in ages gone by
With no telly to tell us or no babies to cry.
Alone by the fireside we'd dream and we'd sit,
Or I'd walk to the gram, and we'd dance to a hit.
Was it Bing, or Nelson Eddy, or John Charles Thomas
When we danced and we whispered and you said that you'd
    promise.
Richard Tauber, Dinah Shore, Donald Peers, Vera Lynn —
We played them and played them until they were thin.

For my sweet Cyclax kiss how you'd coax me and wheedle,
Then back to my arms after changing the needle.
Now, the youngsters have stereo deafened with pop,
They know when to start but they don't know when to stop;
Yet it doesn't seem very far back in the past
When we sat in the lounge making plans meant to last.

No cappuccinos, no discos, no drive-in[2],
We still had a world to be gay and alive in
Now we're happy — perhaps not the world's greatest lovers
With those dusty old records put back in their covers.
But, oh, how we kissed on that very first date
When the old needle hissed on a 78[3].

1970

LAMENT FOR MAID MELBOURNE[1]

The Melbourne of my girlhood was a fine Rexona Town,
Her smile was bright with Kolynos and Persil-white her gown,
Her Bedgegood shoes with Nugget shone, she scorned inferior
  brands,
And in her Lux-white gloves there slept her soft Palmolive
  hands.
She washed her crowning glory in the suds of Wright's Coal
  Tar
And in her spotless laundry lay her loyal Velvet bar;
With Reckitt's Blue (a knob or two), Dutch Cleanser and a
  chamois,
While every window in her house was sparkling with Bon
  Ami.
White Lily kept her bathtub bright, and Silvo shone her tap
And the fragrant scent of Phenyl wafted from her gully trap.

But where, Oh where, I ask you, is that wholesome lass of
  yore?
The Wundawax has long since dimmed upon her kitchen
  floor.
The Marveer on her dining suite is caked with layers of soot
And her Cuticura'd face is black as a Monash student's foot[2].
Her breath where Floral Cachous mingled once with Listerine

Now reeks like New Australian food, or a Harpic-less latrine;
Those stockings washed in Sunlight soap are soaked with mud
    and sweat.
And Aunt Jenny[3] wouldn't recognise her filthy lace layette!
Immaculate Miss Melbourne has really gone to pot,
A foul old crone now occupies John Batman's spotless spot.
She defiles the land we borrowed from the Aborigines,
As I'm sure they would corroborate between corroborees.
Her chimneys stain the Dulux sky, the Yarra is polluted,
In Phillip's Bay floats foul decay, the Mallee has been rooted.
My childhood creek at Moonee Ponds, which once was clean
    and pure,
Now reeks like a New Australian's breath, or like some open
    sewer.

The tourist with his camera and a gold-filled Qantas bag
Who comes to woo Miss Melbourne meets a filthy toothless
    hag!
She reeks of oil and petrol fumes, her skin is clogged with
    grease,
And in the nude she is tattoo'd with BAN THE BOMB and
    PEACE.
The tourist seeks that fresh young girl, alas he seeks in vain,
Her healthy smiling open face is now an open drain.
He seeks her sweet reflection in the Cultural Centre's moat
Where swim the mandarin peels and the Rothman's packets
    float,
He seeks her in the Civic Square and in St Kilda too,

With a squashed up salad sandwich on the instep of his shoe.
But the sun that shines is sickly and the air he breathes is stale
And at night his once-white hankie tells its own revolting tale.

Meanwhile in filthy London town Sir Alexander Downer[4]
Attempts to sell Australia while our wide brown land gets
    browner.
Our White Australia once as white and pure as Brown and
    Polson[5]
Now looks as black and grubby as Paul Robeson or Al Jolson.
How sad that we who led the way in wholesome demolition
In ripping down germ-laden slums should shirk a finer
    mission.
Our Spirit of Progress, which reduced old buildings down to
    dust,
Was meant to kill Bacteria Bill[6] and thwart the National Trust;
But though those hideous landmarks have all been purged by
    Whelan[7],
There still remains a vast terrain for rubbish to congeal in.
How in this Land of Laminex, Dettol and Pinocleen
Can such things be? The things we see and smell are quite
    obscene!

Let us unite in this great fight against Pollution's menace,
Or Melbourne will be filthier than Paris, Rome — or Venice.

1971

TERRIBLY WELL[1]

for Charles Osborne

In the world of success and failure
Have you noticed the genius spark
Seems brightest in folk from Australia?
We all leave an indelible mark.
You just have to go to the Opera
Or an Art show, or glance at your shelves
To see in a trice that Australians
Have done terribly well for themselves.
Joan Sutherland, Rupert Murdoch, Scobie Breasley[2]
Have all pitted themselves 'gainst the Pom,
And the cultural race they've won easily
In spite of the land they come from.
Wilfrid Thomas[3], Germaine Greer, Hammond Innes[4],
To mention a few famous names,
Have all been taken to Old England's bosom
Along with Skippy[5] and Mr Clives James[6].
Did you know that Rolf Harris was Australian?
Peter Finch, Coral Browne, Keith Michell?[7]
All your best dentists come from the Land of the Gum[8]
And they've all done so terribly well.
Evonne Goolagong[9] hails from the outback
The White Hope of Australian sport.
I could sing out our praises all evening

And my list would be still far too short.
You may ask me with ill-disguised envy
Why we Aussies get all the right breaks:
So here is my recipe for world-wide renown:
Mother's love, lots of sun, juicy steaks!

1972

FIRST DAY COVERS

The following group of verse was written by Mrs Everage and set to music by Nigel Butterley. (They are dedicated to those little windows on our way of life — Australian postage stamps.) The work was performed and recorded with the Sydney Symphony Orchestra conducted by John Hopkins.

———— ■ ————

FIRST DAY COVERS

The image of Australia is precious to us all:
Ayer's Rock, the mighty Yarra and the Warringah Shopping
Mall.
It's hard to think our heritage could meet with vile attack
From expatriates who stab the hand who fed them in the back.
That such vile knockers still exist, I do not understand.
It's a very bad advertisement for our wide, brown, sunburnt
land.

So we must prove to foreign nations that we do not think
they're our betters,
And advertise our glories by the stamps stuck on our letters.

Each new Australian issue is a real collector's prize
And I'm told that great philatelists can scarce believe their
eyes.

They reel back stunned, their eyes dilate, their fingers twitch
  and grope
When they behold an Aussie stamp upon an envelope.

So why not use the postage stamp at which we so excelleth,
And thus proclaim the glorious name of our great
  Commonwealeth.
            1972

My Little Philatelist

for Jeffrey Smart

Our son Kenny was an Argonaut[1], Hernia 43,
So naturally we had to listen to the ABC.
It bathed our home in culture, it nourished home and mind
And the culture that it brought us was the patriotic kind.
The Argonauts encouraged Ken along the right direction,
And the little man quite soon began to form a stamp
    collection.
At first I wasn't all that keen, I was inclined to quibble,
To watch that kiddie play with all that dried-up foreign
    dribble.
So we only let him touch his stamps with rubber gloves and
    tweezers,
Just in case some tongue had covered them with horrible
    diseases.
Yet Kenny's hobby is infectious and I get excited too,
When the family's finished brekkie and the morning post is
    due.
The Birko[2] is a-bubbling as I hear the postie's whistle[3]
And through my snail-encrusted slot[4] he pushes his epistle.
Young Kenny scampers down the drive amongst the
    flowering phlox,
And I see him through the louvres as he fumbles at the box.

115

If he finds a precious specimen he's as happy as a pup,
As he opens wide his album and deftly sticks it up.
Other kiddies would be happy, if they only had a penny'th
Of the pleasure that his stamp collection gives to little Kenneth.

1972

THE SHARK STAMP

Australia has its share
Of horrid fish and faunas.
They lurk in sea and air
And in the most unlikely corners.
Yet who are we to slam
The black sheep of Noah's Ark,
For he who made the Lamb
Also made the Grey Nurse Shark.
They romp around our beaches,
You can spot them by their dorsal,
And a second course of torso
Is for them a tasty morsel.

1972

THE BLOWFLY STAMP

Busy little blowflies
Are naughty little wags,
They don't fly as the crow flies
But go by zigs and zags.
They're inclined to spread diseases,
They buzz around like shoppers,
And the junior of the species
Are called Morteiny[1]-boppers.

                                    1972

THE FUNNEL-WEB SPIDER STAMP

Funnel-web spiders are very quick and nimble,
They dance in St Ives and they prance in Pymble.
Sleeping on your pillow slip, in and out the plug,
On the baby's bassinette, beneath the picnic rug.
They choose the most unusual spots to build their little
    bowers,
We'd hate to be in their shoes, but they'd love to be in ours!
Sharks are rather working class, blowflies are a bore —
But funnel-web spiders are frightfully North Shore[1].

1972

PIECE IN THE FORM OF A MEAT PIE

I think that I could never spy
A poem lovely as a pie.
A banquet in a single course
Blushing with rich tomato sauce.
A pie whose crust is oven kissed,
Whose gravy scalds the eater's wrist.
The pastie and the sausage roll
Have not they brown mysterious soul;
The dark-hued Aborigine
Is less indigenous than thee.
Like Phillip Adams[1] rich and chubby,
Tasteful as Patrick White[2],
With an ice-cold Carlton stubbie,
You're the Great Australian Bite.

1972

THE PAVLOVA STAMP

Marie Antoinette of France was a very selfish queen,
It's not surprising that she ended on the guillotine;
She ate rich gâteaux all day long as though she'd never seen
    them,
Though her starving subjects barely had a vanilla slice between
    them.
'Let them eat cake!' she cruelly spake, forgetful of their misery,
But the hungry horde could not afford to shop at her pat-isserie.
So the proud queen was defeated, despite her fine regalia,
But we have our cake and eat it, in heaven-blest Australia!
Pavlovas are a national treat, and lest we grow too greedy
Let's spare a prayer (as we eat) for all the poor and needy.

There's a moral to the pavlova
With its luscious creamy clots —
It's like mankind all over:
The Pavs, and the Pav-nots!
        1972

THE LAMINGTON STAMP

Every nation in creation has its favourite cake.

The French have got their gâteaux, strudel's the German's
 bake.

Scotland has its shortbread, and England has its scone,

But none of them can rival the Australian Lamington.

You'd think at first they were baked in France,

Or some other *haute cuisine* land,

Yet they're named after Lord Lamington,

A Governor of Queensland!

The story goes the Governor in 1896

One day found he was craving for a Betty Sydney Mix[1];

But the cake tin it was empty and he felt his spirits plunge,

There was only chocolate icing so the chef threw in the
 sponge.

Then in despair he climbed a chair with rope to hang himself,

Knocking a tin of coconut down from a topmost shelf.

It sprinkled down upon the cake, the kitchen door did ope.

'What's holding up cook?' the Governor said, then saw that it
 was rope.

Then the Governor, Lord Lamington (known to his friends as
 'Geoff'),

Spied a plate of curious cakes beneath his swinging chef.

He nibbled one, he gobbled two, he quaffed the whole darn
 plateful,

And then revived the hapless cook to tell him he was grateful.
The cook lay on the kitchen floor, a case of strangulation.
And he whispered hoarse the recipe of his fatal last creation.
The grief-crazed Governor placed him in a splendid tomb of
    bronze,
And the story goes that he laid a wreath of luscious lamingtons.

1972

SURFERS PARADISE

I'm told that Surfers Paradise was once a dismal hole.
You could take the kiddies for a swim and never see a soul;
There was just a lonely comfort station scribbled with
  obscenities
Now you can hardly see the sea for all the nice amenities!
Lovely motels and mini-golf, Ansett air hostesses,
Double Bay ladies on parade in Paula Stafford dresses.

You're welcome on the Golden Coast to stretch out on your
  Dri-Glos,
Or read the Australasian Post on comfy poolside li-los;
You can lie on the beach in easy reach of your Esky or your
  trannie —
Or share a jug of Tooheys with a mauve-rinsed, Kwik-tanned
  grannie.

We mostly go to Surfers when we need a restful spell,
And Norm and I always like to stay at the Beachcomber
  Motel,
There are little shops nearby which sell all kinds of shells and
  gifts.
And the theme from Dr Zhivago murmurs softly in the lifts.

The place is such a heavenly spot, I hope no one will ruin it —
I only wish we'd had the sense to buy ourselves a unit;
Where the sun shines bright as silicone on the Paradise beneath
On gold bikinis, golden thongs, and lots of golden teeth!

1972

THE GLADDY STAMP

Dear land of mine, Australia,
What symbol stands for thee?
Should it be the Southern Cross,
Or the flowering wattle tree?
A smiling television set,
Or a sprig of nice boronia . . .
Should our final stamp bear the head
Of William
or Sonia[1]?

Beautiful land of sunshine,
Oh, happiest of nations —
Home of the Sydney Opera House
And a million service stations.
What Vision Spendid sums thee up,
Ayer's Rock or a glass of beer?
Should our final stamp bear the head
Of the Queen
or Dr Greer[2]?

And if our enemies threaten us
What should our emblem be —
A Japanese plastic boomerang
Or the head of BHP[3]?

Yet in times of tribulation
Nothing can quite console us,
And fill our hearts with gratitude
Like the Australian . . . gladiolus!

1972

——— ■ ———

LICKING THE BEATERS

for Ken Thomson

When I was a wee girlie,
And brought tea to Mummy early,
Or went shopping on my scooter
For the family veg and meat,
My good deeds were not rewarded
With a coin or something sordid,
But my Mother always saved for me
A truly wondrous treat.
She was always baking sponges,
Whisking eggs with swirls and lunges
Of those little manual beaters
That we used to turn by hand.
And when she finished she would pick them
Up and say: 'Here, Edna, lick them!'
How I loved to lick the beaters
As a kiddie. It was grand!
I confess, as I grew older,
My taste for cake mixtures grew bolder
Till my first electric mixer came along — O wondrous treat!
I loved going on a bender
In the kitchen with my blender
And the golden gooey goodness
Was, to me, both drink and meat.

But I heard a gruesome story
(And I warn you this is gory)
Of a Continental woman
Who I fear had little brains.
She was licking the elixir
From the flanges of her mixer,
But the foolish creature hadn't
Switched the power off at the mains!
The blades began rotating
Where her tongue was undulating,
And soon her gruesome organ
Was wound round and round the whisk.
So don't place much reliance
When you're tonguing your appliance,
For if you accidentally switch it on
You run a ghastly risk.
I remember when young Ken would
Love to lick my gleaming Kenwood.
When I was running up a gâteau
Or a sponge cake or a bun
And even now when I'm cooking
I see big Ken slyly looking
And with a little pang I know
I have a glossophagine son.

1976

DIRGE FOR THE MOONEE PONDS TOWN HALL[1]

I had a dream the other night —
My old town hall had caught alight.
And when I woke I somehow knew
My ghastly nightmare had come true.
I saw the headlines stark and brash:
HISTORIC HALL REDUCED TO ASH.
I heard despairing fireman shout,
'No hose on earth can put this out.'
Grief shrouds me like a smoky pall
Which hangs o'er Moonee Ponds Town Hall.
Does Melbourne realise what it lost
In this appalling holocaust?
I wonder what perverted swine
Would wish to harm this national shrine?
How painfully I now recall
My girlhood days in Moonee's Hall.
Prophetically the Hall was hot
The night I won the Lucky Spot,
And love light burnt and friends were warm
The day I tied the knot with Norm.
Was it some warped and twisted joke

To send our Town Hall up in smoke?
But frankly I get rather cross
To think how few will mourn this loss.
For though tears run down Australian cheeks,
It won't mean quite the same to Greeks . . .[2]

1976

SILVER SONG[1]

for Amy Witting

Many folk have asked me what silver means to me.
My reply to them is simply balls upon a Christmas tree.
I adore the silver tinsel and the silver stars above,
Silver paper round a chocky — all things silvery I love.
Silver is the colour of my Norm's masonic trowel,
Silver the foil I wrap around my family's Sunday fowl.
The horseshoe was of silver that I fondled as a bride,
And when it comes to cold-boiled beef, just give me
    silverside.
Silver's such a soft shade, whereas gold is rather harsh,
And there's silver threads aplenty in my old bridesmaid's
    moustache.
Silver is the chromium rail on which I dry my towels,
Silver is the dribble swinging from a toddler's jowls.
The Rolls Royce is of silver that I've always longed to drive,
And silver were the forceps that helped my little ones arrive.
But the silver Miracle of Science that helped me make this trip
Is the gleaming silver nozzle on my husband's bedside drip.

1977

ODE TO
ANGUS & ROBERTSON[1]

Oh literature I love you,
You're always by my side;
Guess where my eager fingers strayed
On the night I became a bride?
On went the bakelite bedside lamp,
On went my reading specs
As I turned your informative pages
And banished all thoughts of sex.
Not that the slumbering bridegroom
(My wonderful husband Norm)
Hungered so much on that fateful night,
For my trembling sylph-like form;
And now four grandchildren later
His chances get fewer and fewer;
But I'm still propped up between satin sheets
Enjoying literature.
Where are the books I perused of old,
The volumes I loved to probe,
The *White Cliffs of Dover*, *Lust for Life*,
The Snow Goose and *The Robe*?
I used to love *The Big Fisherman*,

But I see now my taste was wrong,
So now I'm into Sylvia Plath
And the works of Erica Jong!
I like committed authors
I adore a relevant read;
I'm not like the rabble, Ms Margaret Drabble
Gives me all the succour I need.
And so it's with patriotic pride
I stand before you today
For a famous Australian publishing house
Had girded itself for the fray.
Angus & Robertson Limited
Has purchased this luxury site —
The vendor thought it would never be bought
Though he prayed the Arabs might.
Here let us pause a moment
Let a hush fall over our chatter —
For soon from this throbbing enterprise
Will flow quality reading matter.
For all the world loves Australia,
And thank goodness it isn't a sin to.
Gents please give me a call
If you see anything at all
You feel like dipping into.
I can feel a little lump rising
And there's goose pimples on my back

To think archaeologists a million years hence
Will poke up my precious plaque.
So charge your glasses, possums,
And drink a grateful toast
To Angus & Robertson Limited
Fine publisher — KIND HOST.

1979

MY PUBLIC[1]

for Liza Minnelli

A cheering crowd at my stage door,
An audience crying out for more —
That's what my public means to me.
The loyal fans who queue for hours
The cards, the telegrams, the flowers,
That's what my public means to me.
You need to have a pretty humble attitude
When you see little faces looking up
Grotesque with gratitude.
So from tiny tots to grannies,
I love all your nooks and crannies —
That's what my public means to me.

The Queen's Birthday Honours List,
This lovely Cartier on my wrist —
That's what my public means to me.
A limousine, a sable coat,
The lump that's rising in my throat —
That's what my public means to me.
Superstars may come and go, but there's no other
That folks identify with their own mother.
To think there's people in this room
Who wish they'd sprung out of my womb —
That's what my public means to me.

The David Hockneys on my wall
The Royal visitors who call —
That's what my public's done for me.
All those requests I get to stay
With famous folk in St Tropez,
For that's their idea of fun for me.
But they can keep Roman Polanski and Bianca,
It's for the company of nobodies like you I hanker.
You're my shelter from the storm
You're all as precious as my Norm —
That's what my public means to me.

ENCORE
And now the time has come to part,
I've got an ache inside my heart —
That's what my public do to me.
While little know-alls squirt their poison,
I can feel my eyelids moisten
When I think how my public still stays true to me.
I may be forced to live in a tax haven
But I know I'm home when I see all those gladdies wavin',
And how could I forsake them
When they raise their stalks and shake them —
That's what my public means to me,
That's what you mean to me.

1979

EDNA'S ACCOLADE

Lucky possum that you are
You are now a mini star!
A big fish in a tiny pond
Thanks to Edna's magic wand.
Timid once, now slightly bolder
Since that gladdy touched your shoulder;
Go forth now, be kind and true
Just like Dame Edna was to you —
May love and laughter always blossom
Now that you're a life-long possum!

1980

VESPERS

for my godson Earl McGrath

Megastar kneels at the foot of the bed,
Droops on the Santos watch wisteria head.
Hush! Hush! Whisper who dares!
Dame Edna Everage is saying her prayers.

God bless Madge. I'm feeling woozie.
Wasn't it fun in the new jacuzzi?
Romping around in the bubbling water.
Oh God bless Valmai — my problem daughter.

The nightie I'm kneeling in looks rather naff,
But Kenny my son's huddled over his Pfaff,
Running me up some spunky numbers.
God bless Kenny while he slumbers.

Although he's artistic he's a red-blooded male,
And so is his flatmate, Clifford Smail.
They've hit it off so well together
Since Cliff won his title: Mr Leather.

Oh! Thank you, Dame Nature, for all you've done
For Brucie, my middle-management son.
And thanks for the gladdy which sprouts from the corm,
And I nearly forgot to say God bless Norm.

139

Megastar kneels at the foot of the bed,
Prays for the creature she long ago wed.
If you would interrupt her, then kindly refrain,
Dame Edna is thinking of others again.

1982

EDNA'S PLEA

ASSUME KNEELING MODE.

Lord
As I face the daily storm
Let me not forget my Norm,
Spoilt and wrapped up nice and warm
Prostrate in his hozzie dorm.
Quiescent, like a gladdy corm.
But, if your wonders you perform —
Restoring Norm to shipshape form —
Pray first, Thy Servant, You inform
(for Heaven's sake).

YOU MAY STAND
1982

EDNA'S PRAYER FOR OUR TIME

for Claudia Rosencrantz

LOCK YOURSELF INTO ONGOING KNEELING SITUATION.

Hear my prayer Oh Heavenly Lord,
Make me viable across the board;
May my bottom line be virtue
Lest I ever bug or hurt You,
And help me to unite the nations
In ongoing worship situations.
Uptight and hassled though I be
Help me to be upfront with Thee.
And though my input be minute
When Thou my shortfall dost compute,
Pray let my daily print-out say
Thy servant was relevant per se.

1982

THE MADGNIFICAT
for Madge Allsop

Before I take my forty winks
Pray forgive this wicked minx
Of her conceit I've had a plateful,
Just help her to be faintly grateful.
Perhaps I've given her too much
And now she treats me like a crutch.
Sometimes I fear I'll bend and snap
As selfish Madge tugs on my pap
Of niceness, warmth and generosity,
Pray help me to love this old monstrosity.
She came to me without a cent
And all she owns I gladly lent.
I've pumped, let's face it, telephone numbers
Into her bank. And now she slumbers.
She who was once so lithe and young,
Spare her the rough edge of my tongue.
I should be comforted perhaps
That dear old Madge is under wraps.

1982

A MEGASTAR'S MANTRAS
Things That Mean a Lot to Me

A is for Australia,
The land I adore;
It's so spotless and clean
You can eat off the floor.

B is for Boomerang,
Which our quaint Abos launch
In the hope it will bring back
A roast quokka's haunch.

C is for Culture
Which blossoms unchecked,
You can't move in my homeland
For Beckett and Brecht.

D is for Dingo,
Our indigenous pup,
You just have to look at him
And he'll gobble you up.

E is for Explorer,
A brave little chap
Who helped put my wonderful land
On the map.

F is for Funnel-web
Our furry-legged foe.
He sleeps in your slipper
And breakfasts on toe.

G is for Gladdy, Ginseng, Galle glass,
It's also for Glyndebourne where you eat off the grass.
G stands for Gucci, James Galway, Gay Lib,
Gallipoli, Galliano, and the four brothers Gibb.
The Golden Goanna is our top film award
And with Genet and Günter Grass I'm never bored.
Glenda Jackson and Greta Garbo are Gs without peer,
So are Gough, Gary Glitter and our own Germaine Greer.
To hear Grace Jones sing I'd pay quite a lot for,
And Gaddafi's a socialist I've got a soft spot for.
G stands for Graffiti, a word that I veto
Since Mature Students have taught me to call it Graffito.
By the end of this poem I'm sure you'll agree
That I have a very soft G-spot for G!

H is for Harrods,
My favourite boutique;
If you shop there they'll treat you
Like a little-known sheik.

I is for invalid
Who'll never come home;
I've just given Norm's drip
A new coat of chrome.

J is for Joylene,
My daughter-in-law;
In a jumpsuit she skates
On a black rubber floor.

K is for Kelly
Our radical Ned;
When none other dared
He wore a tin on his head.

L is for Leather
In sling-backs and mules,
You should see the accessories
My son's flatmate tools.

M is for Mould-breaking,
What I do best,
With the mould on Madge Allsop
I'm put to the test.

N is for Nivea
Where my digit oft dives;
Try it in a sandwich
With finely chopped chives.

O is for Opera House,
An Australian invention
Ideal for casino
Or business convention.

P is for Pizzazz
Which makes paupers happy,
They adore my charisma
And I'm raunchy and zappy!

Q is for Queen
Whom I know very well;
She's confided some scorchers
Which I doubt if I'll tell.

R is for Refinement
Which Australians exude,
Don't let some of our statesmen
Persuade you we're crude.

S is for Subsidies
The Arts Council keeps giving,
Thus sparing our authors
From writing books for a living.

T is for Thrush,
The name of a bird;
It's also a yukky old fungus
I've heard.

U is for Urine
Say 'yuk' if you might;
Little jobs keep
Mother's hands soft and white.

V is for Valmai,
My sensitive daughter;
She was uptight in Safeways
When security caught her.

W is for Woodwork
At which Madge is improving,
She keeps me awake
With her tonguing and grooving.

X is for X-ellence,
Though it's not spelt that way;
It's my bottom line
At the end of the day.

Y stands for The Yell,
And I've got a queer hunch
It's the most gorgeous thing
Ever painted by Munch.

Z is for Zero,
A mark I bestow
On once-famous women
Like Margaret Trudeau.

1982

THE FABRIC OF MY LIFE

There's something about my man I'll ne'er forget:
His winceyette[1].
Each night when I turned off our TV set
And crept beneath our old mosquito net,
Into our double bed I'd gently get
And there asleep I'd spy my darling pet
In winceyette.

Now years have passed,
His place there at my flank
Is taken by a form huddled and dank,
Who in the daytime treats me like a bank
And when night falls —
To be completely frank —
Deserves a jolly good old-fashioned spank!

I still wake up beside her damp with sweat
And thoughts gnaw at my being and fancies fret
That Norm so far away is with me yet,
Swathed in that fabric that I'll ne'er forget —
Pure winceyette.

1982

MY DRAWER

Nature is red in tooth and claw
Inside the humble bedside drawer,
Midst soiled buds and cotton balls
The genie of the jungle calls.
When day is done and darkness lingers,
What better place for eager fingers
To fumble, frolic and explore
Than deep within a bedside drawer.

1982

NEW ZEALAND

for Jane Campion

The land that calls itself 'New Zillin'
Says it discovered penicillin,
But it tends to bowl me over
When Kiwis claim that the pavlova
Originated in a pause
For tea during the Maori wars.
We Aussies wouldn't dare dispute
Their just claim to the Kiwi fruit,
But who'd suspect our famed meringue
From a volcanic island sprang?
And yet, observe next time you carve a
Well-cooked pav — it looks like lava!

1983

ODE TO JOHN LAWS[1]

Some say you are impatient,
Some complain that you are rude,
Some declare you always put them
In a controversial mood.
To some your voice is chiding,
You sound old, yet strangely young;
And I've heard you give a hiding
To foolish people with your tongue.
But they say you give wise counsel
And I know you understand,
As you tune into the ground swell
And the grassroots of our land.
There've been times when you have well expressed
Our nation's pent-up fury,
You've talked to everyone from Premiers
To the members of a jury.
Yet every time I hear your show
As I perform my up-market chores,
I think: 'All Australia knows that voice —
But I know the real John Laws.'
I know the man who helps his friends
And never asks for thanks,
The man whose thighs are happiest
Wrapped round a gee-gee's flanks.

A farming man who loves the land,
Each blade of grass and tree;
A thinking man whose favourite task
Is writing poetry.
A ladies' man whose women friends
Betray his perfect taste,
My pals are all astonished
Our relationship is chaste.
But a family man also exists
Within this complex frame,
Justice you love —
For is not Law the best part of your name?
I know you well, your tweedy smell,
The smoke from your cheroot;
The hint of claret on your breath
And the pasta on your suit;
The little touches that make up
The man I long to see,
Edna knows John, perhaps too well,
But does my John know me?
I wonder possums if he does,
Behind the jokes and quips,
Does he resent this killjoy microphone
Betwixt our eager lips?
I doubt if he adores me,
This lanky grown-up elf,
Or are John Laws' emotions
Laws unto himself?

I will survive, my shows are great,
My cup of life is full;
And yet I quiver when I hear
Herb Alpert's 'Lonely Bull'.[2]
You are the Hamlet of the wireless,
Your Ophelia is me.
I helped you make your big decision
'To Be . . . or 2GB[3]'.
He's helped me through my marriage,
Through birth, death and menopause —
Let's all be thankful for the mystery
And the magic of John Laws.

1983

A WISH COME TRUE

Lines for a child's autograph book

When I was at my mother's knee
She asked me what I'd like to be,
But all I said was 'goo ga ga'
(That's baby talk for MEGASTAR).
Now I'm beauteous, rich and wise,
I look at life with older eyes;
And though I am a famous Dame,
Underneath I'm just the same.
Much more compassionate than I look —
That's why I'm writing in this book!
Each night I ask the Lord's advice:
'Please, Possum, why am I so nice?'

Your parents will go mad with glee
If you grow up as nice as me!

1983

ODE TO KOALA BLUE[1]

Today I really feel terrific
For Australian culture has crossed the Pacific.
And thanks to Olivia, my promising niece,
Everyone here can buy a piece.
Here are gorgeous frocks by our top designers
And opals dug up by dusky miners.
There is food that has been passed by our health authorities
And the odd artefact by our ethnic minorities.
There are sweaters as soft as a cockatoo's tuft,
And cuddly koalas humanely stuffed.
For here in LA is a colourful Korner
Inspired by Australian flora and fauna.
Feather and fur and claw and beak —
If it comes from Down Under it's bound to be chic.
I know shoppers will flock here from New York to Dallas
To buy things from the land that makes everyone jealous;
And I hear people whisper as they wander through:
'Is there nothing on earth that Australia can't do?'
It's so safe there and sunny we don't have to think
So our bodies are brown and our Government's pink;
The Australian male is a glamorous hunk,
In defeat he is modest, and in victory — drunk.
Whilst our womenfolk are — as I'm sure you'll agree —
As talented and tasteful as Livvy and me.

1983

ODE TO THE MEDIA

Australia's a wonderful country
Which no one can sully or hurt,
So long as we pray
At the end of the day
To Jana, George, Tony and Bert.[1]

We love all those telly commercials
Which help us stay young and keep clean.
And our age drops to zero
When our media hero
Winks and waves at us out of the screen.

Our mummies sit sucking their vallies
While we bask in the flickering glow.
Our dads scratch their premature bellies
As we're told all Australians need know.

And forgot are the old recreations:
Chess and Scrabble are time-wasting folly,
As Australia the luckiest of nations
Settles down on its knees before Molly.

It's so nice not to go to the theatre,
It's so restful not opening a book,
It's sheer ecstasy
Just eat, sleep and pee
Then to switch on the box and just look.

So thank you to God in your steeple
For a life without aggro or hitch,
And thanks to the Greeks and boat people
For working and making us rich.

It's a wonderful way to avoid all
The sorrows that cause us to frown,
As an ape-man in tones adenoidal
Exhorts everyone, 'Come on down!'

We're coming, wherever you lead us
And we'll grovel about in the dirt,
We just want to know that you need us,
Dear Tony and Darryl and Ray and Jana and George and
    Mike and Brian and
Katrina and Craig and Patti and Derryn and Robbo and
    Molly,
And Bert.
    1983

NOSTALGIE DE LA JEUNESSE

Polyester bearded Santa
Sitting in your fairy cave,
Sipping stronger stuff than Fanta —
Give the kiddies one more wave.
Preach your jolly Christmas sermon
With our toddlers on your knee,
Beneath all that acrylic ermine
It must be Celsius 33.
Derryn got a walkie-talkie,
Vanessa got a brand new pup,
Daddy asked for (and got) Hawkie[1],
Bondy[2] got a silver cup.
Loaded with loot
It's quite appalling
That we'd rape or kill or steal
For one small gift that's past recalling:
The way that Christmas used to feel.

1983

DAME EDNA'S HISTORIC ODE TO BARNARDO'S[1]

When Bruce[2] first ran his chilly tape
From my slender ankle to naked nape
I asked him: 'Of all the girls you've dressed,
Tell me frankly, possum, who's the best?'

Bruce gave me one of his famous grins,
But, alas, his mouth was full of pins.
Yet I doubt if his answer would give you a shock
As you gaze at me now in this stunning frock.

But I must be as generous as I am able
To those poor runners-up in the Oldfield stable —
You all look gorgeous, you've all done your best
And it's not my fault I'm better dressed.

But tonight's event is no mere charade
Of glamour pusses on parade,
And though I'm an actress and 'chantoose',
I've been given a job to do by Bruce.

He said: 'Edna, please write a few talented verses
To make those silly old tarts put their hands in their purses.
It's within your powers as a megastar
To remind us all how lucky we are.'

So as we gobble our champers and avocados
Let's think of the work done by Dr Barnardo's.
And let me tell you my secret for satisfied living:
It's giving and giving and giving and giving.

What a relief to know your donation
Won't be squandered away on administration.
I think of young Bruce as though he's my son,
But if I get too emotional my mascara might run.

So welcome to this Barnardo's beano
(To think I almost wore my Valentino!)
But a spooky voice inside my head
Made me slip into this instead.

And darling Bruce would get such a shock
To spy me in a rival's frock.
But isn't this Oldfield number bliss?
I know women who'd kill to dress like this.

But Bruce's top clients all agree:
It's an honour to be upstaged by me.
Yet the Barnardo's boys and girls we know
Are the real stars of this glittering show.

With our generous help their feet will be planted
On the road of life we took for granted.
So turn your minds possums, from food and sex,
The fashion tonight is big fat cheques!

1984

I CAN'T LET
MY PUBLIC DOWN[1]

A second ago I was locked in my room,
My life seemed pointless and hollow
When it used to be warm
With the presence of Norm
And I thought where he's gone I must follow.

I looked at the valium,
I considered the stove,
I weighed up the stern moral issues:
But the strength inside me grew
When I was almost through
My last box of Kleenex tissues.
So I hope you'll all applaud my great achievement:
I'm here tonight in spite of my bereavement.

CHORUS
They said 'Stop the show' but I said 'No!
I can't let my public down.'
They said 'Listen to reason, cancel the season!'
As I put on my widow's gown.
But all you faithful possums
Had queued all over town,
No grief would be too great for me
To let you down.

To think that Norm is still slightly warm
Is hard for me to bear,
On top of that I was worried what hat
What frock, what gloves to wear.
With Barry Humphries in the wings,
Prepared to wreck my song,
But I have to strut my stuff on stage
Where I belong.

And now at last Norm's a thing of the past,
A fragrant memory.
He's in the Twilight Zone and I'm all alone
But at least there's still you and me.
The doctors can keep their sedation,
I'm going to paint the town.
By now you know I'm too much of a pro
To let my public down!

1985

ODE TO REGENT STREET[1]

Possums, it's a very special treat
For me to light up Regent Street.
My predecessors all have been
Quite close relations of the Queen;
Though once Joan Collins threw the switch —
She wasn't Royal, but she was rich.
This year, the Regent Street Committee
Decided it would be a pity
If this event became a farce,
'Invite,' they said, 'someone with class.
Nancy Reagan would be nice
And Mother Teresa's asked us twice.'
To which the Chairman was heard to say,
'Another commoner? No way!'
So that is how the powers that be
Unanimously hit on me,
And tonight my subjects loyal
Can welcome back another Royal,
Although I'm not dripping with regalia
I happen to be the Queen of Australia.
Yet I love London town like you,
Call me old-fashioned, but I do,
And Regent Street is just the best —

That costume jewel on London's breast.
One spot on earth I find it hard
To live without my credit card.
Here eager shoppers flow and ebb
Past Hamleys Toy Shop, Mappin and Webb;
This street fills every human need
From Aquascutum to Austin Reed,
Henrys for purses, Garrards for rocks,
Laura Ashley and Jaeger for gorgeous frocks,
Dickins and Jones, Burberry and Dunn
And British Airways to fly to the sun.
Tower Records is a new arrival,
And Libertys, a chic survival;
Peter Robinson, Wedgewood and Mr Boot
Are just some of the stores on this famous route.
Frankly, possums, my pulse rate quickens,
At the very thought of Jones and Dickins.
No wonder psychiatrists agree
You can't beat retail therapy.
There's pressie buying without tears
Beneath these spooky chandeliers.
What are those baubles hung on high?
Up-market earrings in the sky.
And so on this crisp November night
Dame Edna says, 'Let there be light!'

1989

ODE TO HARRODS[1]

for Mohamed Al-Fayed

I'm thrilled to hear you clap and cheer,
And say what's Edna doing here?
Admittedly it's quite a coup —
I'm standing here in front of you!
By night I do my famous show,
By day I keep my profile low.
Yet though I'm frankly far from poor
I'm first in line at Harrod's door.
But, possums, please don't start to think
I'm just here to buy a bargain mink,
Or snap up some cut-price diamond rings —
I've quite enough up-market things!
No, please ignore that ugly rumour,
I'm not here as a mere consumer
To stockpile satin underwear.
I'm here at dawn 'because I care'!
The things that have made Britain great:
The Cashmere Scarf, the Wedgwood Plate,
Irish Linen, the Shetland Sweater
Are things no other land does better.
And all these gorgeous things and more
Are assembled in this store.
Your heart's desire you here will find

At prices that will blow your mind.
I love this land of Queens and Kings.
Frankly, I'm into English things;
Shakespeare is my favourite bard,
I adore the Trouping of the Guard!
Yet Crufts and Henley come and go,
As does the Chelsea Flower Show.
But all these institutions pale
Beside the mighty Harrod's sale.
This is no place for counter-hopping,
Today's the day for Serious Shopping,
No room for idle browsing gawpers
And certainly no place for paupers!
So gird your loins up, set your jaws
As you surge through these famous doors.
I hope you all emerge serene
With carrybags of gold and green.
I'd rather rise above the fight,
Take my time, and spend the night
Far from those bargain-hunting screams,
I'd drift off into blissful dreams.
Snuggled in my Harrod's bed,
Tucked in by raunchy Mr Al-Fayed.
So go forth, possums, that's my cry,
The sale is open — Buy! Buy! Buy!

1989

DAME EDNA'S
MEGA PLATE[1]

Remember as kiddies locked in our highchairs
We spooned our Farex till we saw the bears?
Each mouthful brought them nearer to our gaze,
Those printed bears of happy childhood days.
Now, thanks to Cranbrook and a Benefactor,
Your plate's embellished with a world-famed actor,
The answer to a true collector's wish
My dishy look immortal on a dish
It's sure to get your gastric juices surging
To eat and watch my gorgeous face emerging.
Be sure to buy a safe to keep this dish in
It's priceless — and a limited edition!

1990

ODE TO THE WESTON AND LOIS WEEDON FLOWER SHOW[1]

for Francis and Susanna Sitwell

My name is Dame Edna and I want you to know
I'm thrilled to be opening this wonderful show.
Like my Northants possums, I've my Saturday best on
To celebrate the botanical glories of Weston.
But I know what you're thinking, I've heard people say:
What's a megastar doing in our village today?
What's a warm caring woman who earns telephone numbers
Doing stuck in a tent fondling giant cucumbers?
Possums, let me tell you it's not what you think,
But my folks and the Sitwells have a spooky old link:
My two boys are not poets, I'll have to confess,
But Kenny, my son, made this beautiful dress.
And Brucie, my eldest (and I say this with pride),
Hasn't written a book, but he could if he tried.[2]
As for me, I'm no ordinary mother and wife,
I was Dame Edith Sitwell in a previous life.
The resemblance is spooky, the evidence ample,
Take this beautiful poem that I wrote, for example.
The rings on my fingers, my way-out sense of fashion,
When people who knew her see me they go ashen.

But reincarnation's a subject we're not all agreed on,
Instead, let's praise the gardeners of Weston and Weedon.
What fuchsias, what ericas, what a huge yellow dahlia,
I'm amazed that such big ones grow outside Australia.
Your cakes and canaries, your budgies and leeks
You have fattened and fed them these long summer weeks,
Till today on their trestles for the whole world to see
Are the fruits of Northampton in a marquee.

When the clouds of war gathered in a sky black as coal,
Cecil Middleton[3] started it — God rest his soul.
His voice on the wireless in tones grave yet gay
Taught the British to dig and keep Hitler at bay.
His message was urgent, which you acted upon,
And you're still digging for victory fifty years on.
So praise to you all on your gold jubilee —
And how lucky you are it's being opened by me!

1990

THE CRANBROOK STEINWAY[1]

for Sheila Cammidge

When I was a schoolgirl back in dear old Moonee Ponds
I had no fairy godmothers to wave their magic wands.
My music teacher told me that my talent was unique
And I eagerly awaited piano lessons once a week.
But there was nobody to subsidise my extra music courses,
So I learnt quite early to fall back upon my own resources.
I did the dishes and I helped my mum with Electrolux and
 mop
And twice a week I helped out in the local corner shop;
I even, like a tomboy, did some weekly paper rounds
Till the pennies that I saved up at last grew into pounds.

One day when I'd accumulated quite a bit of cash
I took the tram to Melbourne to the store of Mr Brash.
There were wonderful pianos in shining tinkling rows
And I smiled up at the salesman and said, 'Wrap me one of
 those.'
He looked down at my outstretched palm and gave a cruel
 laugh,
'You'll never buy a Steinway with a guinea and a half.'
He made me feel just like a pauper in the back streets of
 Karachi,
But secretly I muttered, 'Eat your heart out Liberace.'

I flounced out of Mr Brash's with hot tears in my eyes
For I knew one day I'd give the world a really big surprise;
For a gypsy read my teacup once and told me I'd go far,
She looked into the dregs and said: 'I see a megastar.'
So sadly yet defiantly, back to school I went,
But how was I to practise without a decent instrument?

There was no encouragement at home, my music teacher was
    a Gorgon,
So I began to fantasise about our local vicar's organ.
I had to get my hands on it and so at night I crept
Through a side door of our parish church whilst most of
    Moonee slept.
What chords my little fingers struck, what technique and what
    style,
I little knew the local police were creeping up the aisle;
They took me home and told my mum and packed me off to
    bed,
'Don't let me catch you near a keyboard,' was all my father
    said.
He meant well, my grey-faced daddy, for how was he to
    know
That he'd nipped my talent in the bud before it could properly
    grow.

Now I'm a world-famed megastar as that gypsy said I'd be,
I try to help young people much less fortunate than me.
I see all those little Cranbrook boys like upmarket Tom
    Sawyers

And pray that they won't all turn out to be businessmen and
    lawyers.
And if there's a spark of inspiration in some little schoolboy's
    breast
And he wants to learn the piano, let him practise on the best!
Now Ascham have a Steinway and very smug they are —
Is it right to fob poor Cranbrook off with a little Yamaha?
That girl's school thinks they've kicked a goal with a gift from
    Kerry P,
But though Ascham may have Packer — lucky Cranbrook has
    got me!
    1991

NOTES ON THE POEMS

THE BALLAD OF CHARLES BLACKMAN

1. Recited in honour of my friend Charles Blackman in a Chinese restaurant in Wardour Street, Soho.
2. A reference to the above-mentioned restaurant.
3. Blackman was at this time working on large pictures in charcoal.
4. Bryan Robertson, art critic, art gallery director and early champion of Australian painting.

BOYD SONG AT EVENTIDE

1. Lines on the occasion of Arthur Boyd's historic One Man Exhibition at the Whitechapel Art Gallery, London, circa June, 1962.

AN ODE TO THE CITY OF CAMBERWELL

1. First published in the Camberwell Free Press and later repudiated by the mayor.

UNTITLED SONG FOR THE SIXTIES

1. **title** the right to ownership of property.

ODE TO THE SKIPPING GIRL

1. These verses commemorate the restoration of a famous Melbourne neon sign advertising Skipping Girl vinegar.

2. A beloved Melbourne wrecking family.

3. Little Audrey was the name of the child who inspired her neon counterpart.

ODE TO THE NEW NINE-BY-FIVE

1. Verses launching an exhibition at the Rosalind Hollinrake Gallery, Melbourne, to commemorate the first Australian impressionist exhibition in August 1889 when most of the pictures were painted on cigar lids measuring nine inches by five.

2. Ethnic fuel deracinated from the mallee region.

3. Builders of popular suburban villas.

4. Nicknames for Streeton, Roberts and Conder, Australian impressionists, later much sought after by *Nouveau Riche* collectors.

5. Henry Bolte, comparatively distinguished Premier of Victoria (1955 to 1972), and keen advocate of lassez faire excavation.

6. To 'dip the lid': to raise the hat as a mark of respect, in the manner of C. J. Dennis's characters.

ODE TO THE QUEEN VICTORIA BUILDING, SYDNEY

1. The nocturnal demolition of buildings is common practice in Australia to avoid inconvenient demonstrations by conservationists and lovers of Australia's architectural heritage, e.g. the destruction of the Bellevue Hotel, Brisbane.

WATTLE PARK BLUES

1. Mercurochrome, a bright yellow and antiseptic palliative for grazed knees.
2. Dixies were cylindrical ice cream receptacles of wax paper.
3. **to shout** *Colloq.* to treat, to buy for, to pick up the tab for.

ODE TO THE MELBOURNE THEATRE COMPANY

1. Performed by the author, a former company member, on the occasion of the director John Sumner's retirement.
2. Gladys Moncrieff, Max Oldaker, Cyril Ritchard — distinguished actors, singers and matinee idols of yesteryear.
3. The firm of Ernest Hillier produced a box of chocolates three feet long for theatrical use.
4. Frank Thring, celebrated Australian actor (b. 1926).
5. John Sumner, *éminence grise* of Melbourne Theatre.

ODE TO THE MELBOURNE GRAMMAR SCHOOL

1. Ora et Labora — the motto of Melbourne Grammar School.
2. Dennis Farrington, a famous Melbourne band leader, happily still with us.
3. The only remembered utterance of Malcolm Fraser, Prime Minister of Australia (1975 to 1983), who was no stranger to discomfort.

JUBILEE BLUES

1. Composed after a birthday dinner kindly hosted by the journal *Quadrant*.

2. 'Nifty' is the soubriquet of a provincial functionary of yesteryear.
3. Venerated Australian television personalities.

A PROLOGUE TO THE FIFTIES

1. Recited as a prologue to the life and death of Sandy Stone. First performed at the Atheneum Theatre, Melbourne, 11 November 1990.
2. John O'Keefe and Little Pattie, popular crooners in the rock'n'roll idiom.
3. The Sydney Opera House and function centre, optimistically designed by Joern Utzon.
4. A charming Sydney *flâneur* and arbiter of taste; therefore much in demand.

JOURNO

1. A gentrified Dockside purlieu.

THRENODY FOR PATRICK WHITE

1. Bea Lillie, celebrated review artiste.
2. Douglas Byng (1893–1987) cabaret performer and female impersonator.

TYCOONS

1. Gifted artists whose works were mandatory on the walls of the Australian *nouveaux riches*.
2. An island on the Barrier Reef favoured by parvenus.

EARL'S COURT BLUES

1. First performed on a *Private Eye* record.
2. Earl's Court, a district of London at that time favoured by anglophobic expatriate Australians.
3. **tight** *Colloq.* inebriated; e.g. tight as a tick
4. **feature** obsolete Australian slang for sexual dalliance.

AUSTRALIAN REPARTEE

1. First performed by Barry Crocker in his eponymous role in *Barry McKenzie Holds His Own*.

THE YARTZ

1. First recited as a prologue to the show 'At Least You Can Say You've Seen It'. 'The Yartz' was Australian bureaucratese for the finer things of life.
2. Pioneer usage of 'in terms of' by Sir Les.

ODE TO CONSERVATION

1. This verse commemorates Sir Les's participation in anti-mining demonstrations, when he marched alongside Patrick White and Jack Mundey.

MADAME TOSSHARD'S WAXWORKS

1. Delivered to the British media on the occasion of the installation of Dame Edna's effigy in Madame Tussaud's Wax Museum in Baker Street, London (the first Australian thus represented).
2. An absurd and short-lived institution in London, intended

to promote interest in Australian culture and to employ
superannuated academics.

CAMBRIDGE COUPLETS
1. Lines delivered by Sir Les on the occasion of his investiture
   with an honorary doctorate of Arts and Letters at
   Cambridge University.
2. 'Brideshead Revisited', a popular TV apologia for academic
   effeminacy, based on Evelyn Waugh's book.

ODE TO PARKY
1. Michael Parkinson, whilom British television interlocutor
   on whose programme this panegyric was first delivered.

ODE TO THE MERLIN COMPLEX
1. Recited at the launching of a magnificent new hotel in
   Perth, WA, since refurbished and renamed.
2. The renovation of kitchens is now the only employment
   open to Australian architects.

ODE TO CAIRNS
1. Declaimed by Sir Les Patterson at the official opening of the
   Cairns (Kenz, Kanz) International Airport.

IN TERMS OF MY NATURAL LIFE
1. 'In terms of' was an irritating and ubiquitous locution of the
   mid–1980s.

SALUTE TO EDNA

1. Delivered on Australian television as a prologue to the seminal Australian audience with Dame Edna.

DR SIR LES PATTERSON'S PRESS CLUB EPIC

1. First performed at the National Press Club, Canberra in October 1985.
2. Australian rhyming slang for booze.
3. Shelter shed, a weatherboard structure in the grounds of State Schools, behind which many students received further education.
4. A likeable but ill-favoured Australian politician.
5. Dame Joan Sutherland — Australian diva.
6. An awe-inspiring Australian government official to whom serious complaints about the improper conduct of public officers may be addressed.
7. To 'cark it' is slang for 'to die'.
8. A once-fashionable painter of boardroom landscapes.
9. A high-minded Australian journal, now defunct and forgotten.
10. Superseded regional functionaries of the eighties.
11. A reference to the ex-Australian treasurer the Right Hon. Paul Keating's unpopular measures to render the traditional business lunch non tax-deductible.

ODE TO THE SMH GOOD FOOD GUIDE

1. Intoned by Sir Les Patterson at a dignified function to launch the *Sydney Morning Herald* gourmet guide.

2. The Right Hon. Paul Keating, ex-Australian treasurer introduced unpopular measures to render the traditional business lunch non tax-deductible.

ODE TO 'THE BIG COOK BOOK'

1. Cited by Sir Les at the launching of an edition of drawings and writings by the gifted Australian humourist Patrick Cook.
2. Max Gillies, prodigiously gifted Australian actor and political impersonator/satirist.
3. Two overseas artists of olden days.
4. The *National Times*, a now defunct Australian journal.

LES PATTERSON'S POETIC ADDRESS TO THE PRESS

1. Delivered in the foyer of the Theatre Royal, Drury Lane to publicise *An Evening's Intercourse With Barry Humphries*.
2. Australia House.
3. The distinguished theatre critic of the *Daily Mail* who once had the temerity to qualify his praise of one of Dame Edna's performances.

MAROAN

1. For a reason no-one understands the word maroon has traditionally been mispronounced in Oceania.

EDNA'S HYMN

1. The coda from one of Mrs Everage's songs.
2. Dame Nellie Melba, famous Melbourne diva.

3. A popular singer and pugilist.

THE TURNTABLE OF LIFE
1. An ethnic fuel deracinated from the red soil of the Mallee region in Victoria.
2. The drive-in cinema at which motorists could attend movies without leaving their cars was in its heyday during this period.
3. A 78 was a shellac disk which revolved at 78 revolutions per minute on a felt-covered turntable.

LAMENT FOR MAID MELBOURNE
1. Recited by Mrs Everage at the Melbourne launch by the Right Honourable R. J. Hawke of Whitelock's *A Dirty Story* — a book about pollution in Melbourne.
2. Monash University in this epoch was notable for its tatterdemalion hippie element.
3. Aunt Jenny, a fervent advocate of Persil soap powder, was impersonated by an attractive Sydney actress and appeared frequently on radio and in women's magazines comparing her pristine sheets, towels and tablecloths with her neighbour's grubby napery.
4. Australian High Commissioner in London from 1964 to 1972.
5. The manufacturers of white flour.
6. A popular cartoon representation of a germ, often coloured green, in the *Australian Women's Weekly*.
7. A famous family of wreckers.

TERRIBLY WELL

1. First recited by Mrs Everage at an international poetry forum at the Festival Hall, London in the presence of Allen Ginsberg and W. H. Auden.
2. A celebrated jockey.
3. A famous broadcaster.
4. A notable Australian author.
5. A television marsupial.
6. Autobiographer and wag.
7. Expatriate Australian actors.
8. During this period London was the mecca for Australian dentists.
9. Australian tennis player.

MY LITTLE PHILATELIST

1. A popular radio children's club inspired by Greek mythology.
2. A metal jug fitted with an electrical element.
3. Postmen in these happier days wore uniforms, delivered early on bicycles and announced their arrival at one's letterbox by a polite blast on their whistles.
4. Letterboxes in Melbourne are traditionally the preferred habitat of these ubiquitous molluscs.

THE BLOWFLY STAMP

1. Mortein — a popular insecticide of the period.

The Funnel-web Spider Stamp

1. *Atrax robustus* infests Sydney's otherwise uninteresting northern suburbs.

Piece in the Form of a Meat Pie

1. Phillip Adams — a prosperous and oracular causerist of the period.
2. Patrick White — a venerated misanthrope and author.

The Lamington Stamp

1. A popular packaged cake mix.

The Gladdy Stamp

1. The Right Honourable William McMahon (Prime Minister of Australia from 1971 to 1972) and his wife Sonia.
2. Germaine Greer, celebrated thinker and feminist of the period.
3. Broken Hill Proprietary Limited, a powerful mining consortium.

Licking the Beaters

1. Inspired by a true newspaper report of a glossal amputation in France.

Dirge for the Moonee Ponds Town Hall

1. In 1976 Moonee Ponds Town Hall burnt down. In the Château Marmont hotel in Los Angeles Dame Edna was inspired to write these poignant stanzas.

2. The suburb of Dame Edna's youth now boasts a large Eastern Mediterranean population.

SILVER SONG
1. Performed in the presence of Her Majesty the Queen in Windsor Great Park in February 1977.

ODE TO ANGUS & ROBERTSON
1. Delivered by Dame Edna at the launch of the Angus & Robertson office in London.

MY PUBLIC
1. One of Dame Edna's most requested songs.

THE FABRIC OF MY LIFE
1. A plain-weave cotton fabric with slightly raised two-sided nap.

ODE TO JOHN LAWS
1. An oracular Sydney broadcaster.
2. Mr Laws' evocative signature tune.
3. 2GB Mr Laws' once favoured network.

ODE TO KOALA BLUE
1. Dame Edna's tribute to her god-daughter Olivia Newton John, recited in Melrose Avenue, Los Angeles, at the opening of her Emporium — Koala Blue.

ODE TO THE MEDIA
1. Adored Australian television personalities of the epoch.

NOSTALGIE DE LA JEUNESSE
1. R. J. Hawke, Prime Minister of Australia (1983 to 1991).
2. Alan Bond, former tycoon and winner of the America's Cup.

DAME EDNA'S HISTORIC ODE TO BARNARDO'S
1. Performed in the ballroom of the Grosvener House in the presence of HRH Princess Diana at a charity event to raise money for the Barnardo's Boys Homes.
2. Bruce Oldfield, celebrated couturier and former Barnardo's Boy.

I CAN'T LET MY PUBLIC DOWN
1. Lyrics of a song, commemorating her husband's death, sung by Dame Edna in the show *Tears Before Bedtime*, 1985.

ODE TO REGENT STREET
1. Recited before Dame Edna performed the historical service of switching on the Christmas lights in Regent Street in November 1989.

ODE TO HARRODS
1. Dame Edna opened the Harrod's sale at the request of the Chairman Mr Mohamed Al-Fayed.

DAME EDNA'S MEGA PLATE

1. Lines inscribed on a beautiful plate sold for the benefit of Cranbrook School in Sydney.

ODE TO THE WESTON AND LOUIS WEEDON FLOWER SHOW

1. Recited on the lawn at Weston Hall, home of the poet Sir Sacheverell Sitwell, to open their famous flower show.
2. The frequent boast of many Australians, though fewer express the intention of composing string quartets.
3. A famous British wartime broadcaster and horticulturist.

THE CRANBROOK STEINWAY

1. Lines delivered at the Regent Hotel in Sydney in February 1991 to raise money for a Steinway piano for the pupils of Cranbrook School. The sister school, Ascham, already had a valuable instrument donated by the philanthropist Kerry Packer, Esquire.

STREET MAP
OF MELBOURNE

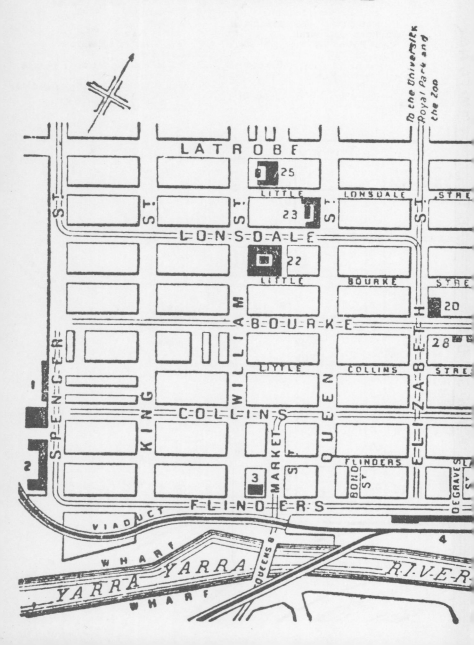